MOTOR CYCLE REPAIR AND UPKEEP

*A Comprehensive, Practical and Authoritative Guide
for the Owner - Driver and Garage Mechanic*

General Editor
EDWARD MOLLOY
Gold Medallist, King's Prizeman in Applied Mechanics

Advisory Editor
J. EARNEY, M.I.M.T.

CONTRIBUTORS

J. EARNEY, M.I.M.T.	STANLEY GREENING, A.M.I.A.E.
W. S. BANNER	LEON GRIFFITHS, A.M.I.E.E., A.M.I.A.E.
Lt.-Col. D. J. SMITH, O.B.E., M.I.A.E.	A. E. FIELD
B. P. RANSOM	F. A. CONEY
T. L. WILLIAMS	EDWARD HILL
S. A. NEWTON	H. G. GALE
B. F. C. FELLOWES	E. W. KNOTT, M.I.A.E.
J. H. KELLY	W. STEVENS
A. F. HOULBERG	S. GILL
W. C. HAYCRAFT	E. F. CHIDLEY
C. A. ELMHIRST BOOKER, M.Sc.(Eng.)	L. C. STIRMAN
DONALD S. PARSONS	B. BOURKE

GEORGE NEWNES LIMITED
SOUTHAMPTON ST., STRAND, LONDON, W.C.2

Published by
classicmotorcyclemanuals.com 2013

Stephen Brown April 2013

ISBN 978-1-908890-06-1

Reproduced by Shore Books and Design
Blackborough End, Norfolk PE32 1SF

SPECIAL MACHINES AND COMPONENTS DEALT WITH IN THE WORK

Ariel.	Douglas.
B.S.A.	Matchless.
A.J.S.	Scott.
P. & M.	Sunbeam.
Norton.	Triumph.
Levis.	J.A.P. Engines.
New Hudson.	Villiers Engines.
Raleigh.	Sturmey-Archer Gearbox.
Velocette.	Burman Gearbox.
Royal Enfield.	Amal Carburetter.
New Imperial.	Amac Carburetter.
Rudge.	Villiers Carburetter.
Calthorpe.	Binks Carburetter.

CONTENTS

iii

CONTENTS

CONTENTS

CONTENTS

The following Timing Charts are included in this work :
B.S.A., MATCHLESS, RALEIGH, RUDGE, A.J.S., J.A.P., ROYAL ENFIELD, SUNBEAM, BLACKBURNE, ARIEL, NORTON, DOUGLAS, NEW IMPERIAL and P. & M. Motor-Cycles.

Introduction to this edition

'Motorcycle Repair and Upkeep' was originally published as a Series of 14 weekly parts around 1932. The complete set of magazines gave useful information and photos on overhauling a number of marques of the period as well as details on various components such as Sturmey Archer & Albion Gearboxes and also provided comprehensive timing charts.

I have decided to republish the 14 parts as a set of 3 books.

Book One Parts 1-4

Articles on; JAP, Levis, Rudge, Scott, Raleigh Engines and Sturmey Archer Gearboxes as well as articles on Brakes, Timing and Decarbonising plus a complete index.

Book Two Parts 5-9

Articles on; Velocette OHC, Sunbeam, Norton Engines, Albion Gearboxes, Ignition & Magnetos, Spark Plugs, Dynamos and Cut Outs, Electric Lamps, batteries and Cables, Instruments and Switches, Cylinder Repairs & Pistons plus a complete Index.

Book Three Parts 10-14

Articles on; BSA, Royal Enfield, P & M, Douglas, AJS, Ariel, Matchless, New Imperial, Villiers, Calthorpe Engines and Rudge, Velocette, BSA, Scott, Burman gearbox and clutches, Con Rod Repairs, Crankshafts, Ignition, Lubrication and a complete Index

Motorcycle Repair and Upkeep 1930 is part of a Series of Vintage Motorcycle books republished by classicmotorcyclemanuals.com. They are; 'Motor Bicycle Building 1906', 'The Motorcyclist's Handbook 1911', 'The ABC of the Motorcycle 1912', 'Motorcycles, Sidecars and Cyclecars 1915', 'Motorcycles in a Nutshell 1923', 'Motorcycling for Women 1928'.

Thank you for buying this book. The publication of such early books is not an easy business and any profits go into the production of the next book in the Series.

By virtue of their high quality and very small print runs these reprinted books are destined to become collector's items in the future.

Thanks again to Nigel for his work on this book and to all those who have given me such positive feedback on the all of the books republished by classicmotorcyclemanuals.com. I hope you find 'Motorcycle Repair and Upkeep' useful.

Steve Brown
classicmotorcyclemanuals.com July 2013

ACKNOWLEDGEMENTS

Thanks to Elsevier Ltd for their kind permission to use this material. This book is reprinted from 'Motorcycle Repair and Upkeep' 1932 Parts 1-4, pages 1-196 (plus index).

General Editor Edward Molloy, Advisory Editor J. Earney.

Contributors to Parts 1-4.

Overhauling a Motorcycle and How to Use a Timing Disc by J. Earney. 3-24
Repair Notes on Levis Engines by W S Banner. 25-44
Decarbonising your Engine by Lieut-Col. D. J. Smith OBE. 45-69
Repair and Maintenance of Rudge Engines by B. P. Ransom. 70-77
General Notes on Dismantling by J. Earney. MIMT. 78-90
The Sturmey Archer Gearbox by T. L . Williams and S. A. Newton. 91-113
Repairs and Adjustments to the Raleigh Engine by T. L. Williams and B. F. C. Fellowes. 103-114
Special Hints on Scott Engines by J H Kelly. 115-128
Brakes and Braking by A. F. Houlberg. 129-157
Engine Noises and What They Tell by WC Haycraft 158-160
Repairing and Overhauling JAP Engines by Stanley Greening. 161-183
Valve and Valve Guide Repairs by Lieut-Col. D. J. Smith OBE. 184-196

INTRODUCTION

IN the past garage men and motor-cyclists have had to gain their practical knowledge of motor-cycle repair work either from experience—a costly process—or by gleaning scraps of information from various publications which devote a small amount of space to this very important subject. Here is a work which is devoted exclusively to the repair and upkeep of motor-cycles.

Many of the repair processes dealt with are, of course, common to all makes of machines. As examples may be mentioned the processes of Decarbonising and Valve Grinding, the Repair of Wheels and Tyres, Carburetter Tuning, Ignition Troubles and Remedies, but as the variation in design of motor-cycles is so great, it was realised by the Editors that a purely general treatment of the various subjects would not be entirely satisfactory. It would, for instance, be almost impossible to compile a series of purely general articles which would be equally applicable to such widely different machines as the " Levis," the " B.S.A." and the " Scott." The only method of compiling a really satisfactory work was to include, in addition to the general articles dealing with usual repair operations, a series of special articles giving just those hints and tips which are so valuable when a garage mechanic or an owner driver is engaged in the dismantling, repair and reassembly of some particular make of machine.

It was felt that the best way to produce this work would be to enlist the co-operation of practical repair men who were familiar with the particular snags likely to be met with in repairing each machine. Very fine contributions have been obtained from practical experts connected with the makers of almost all popular models.

Several contributors give recommended compression ratios, special cams, timing details, and invaluable data on tuning for racing. The complete work forms, in fact, a veritable Encyclopædia of Motor-cycle Repair.

The first of these special sections begins on page 25, and deals with the Levis two-stroke and four-stroke engines. This article gives a good example of the manner in which other engines and special components will be dealt with. That is to say—each of these articles will be packed with practical hints and tips designed to enable repair work on particular machines to be carried out in the minimum of time and in a manner which has been found by experts to be the most satisfactory.

It will be found as the work proceeds that very little space has been devoted to purely theoretical considerations, as there are already in existence several works dealing with that side of the subject. The present work is definitely intended for the man who wishes to repair and adjust motor-cycles either in the home garage or in the course of his everyday work.

A feature which will make a special appeal to the practical man is a series of timing charts which have been compiled for this work from data received from the respective manufacturers. With the aid of these charts the professional repairer will have no difficulty in retiming practically any motor-cycle engines now in use. The private owner will also find them very interesting. It is not recommended that he should disturb the timing of his machine unless there is good reason to suspect that it is at fault, but the charts, used in conjunction with an engine timing disk, will enable him rapidly to check the valve and ignition timing and so ensure that his machine is working at maximum efficiency.

We wish to thank all the firms who have assisted us in connection with the illustrations by giving facilities for special photographs to be taken in their repair and service depots. Special thanks are due to Messrs. Motormyles, Ltd., and to Messrs. Godfreys, Ltd., both of whom gave us great help in the staging of a large number of works photographs covering several makes of machines.

The scope of the present work may be described in a few words by saying that it has been written entirely by practical men for the practical man, with the intention that the wealth of information which has been brought together on this important subject will prove to be of real use both to the mechanically minded motor-cyclist and to the man to whom motor-cycle repairing is part of the day's work.

J. E.
E. M.

OVERHAULING A MOTOR-CYCLE

EXPLAINING HOW TO EXAMINE A MACHINE QUICKLY BUT SYSTEMATICALLY TO DISCOVER ANY WEAK POINTS

By J. Earney, M.I.M.T.

Fig. 1.—The First Thing to do.

Start the engine, using the kick-starter. She should start on the first or second kick. If this is not the case, there are several possible causes, most of which will be detected later in the examination. It is important to remember, however, that magneto trouble is sometimes a cause of difficult starting.

A FEW notes on " vetting " a motor-cycle will be of interest to both the owner who, after a hard season's use, proposes a general over-haul of his machine, and the prospective purchaser of a second- or many-hand model. In the latter case a few systematic tests may mean all the difference between making a good or bad bargain.

STATIONARY TESTS

First start the Engine

It is not possible to get a true test of the cylinder compression with a cold gummy engine, therefore first of all start the engine. In doing so

3

Fig. 2.—A GLANCE AT THE CONTACT-BREAKER POINTS.
Before stopping the engine to make the compression test (Fig. 3), remove the cover of the contact breaker, and notice whether there is excessive sparking at the contact points. If so, expect trouble later.

Fig. 3.—TESTING FOR COMPRESSION.
This is best made with the engine warm. Open the throttle and air, and stand on the kick-starter so that the " compression " can be felt. If the compression disappears quickly suspect worn piston or rings, scored cylinder or leaky valves.

note how easily this is done : difficult starting may be due to a number of causes, among which may be magneto trouble.

Look and Listen

Allow the engine to warm up gradually, meanwhile noting if the oiling system is working and if the engine responds to the ignition control. When this is retarded the exhaust note should become dull and heavy, and the engine appear to be sluggish, but it should speed up immediately the ignition is advanced again. Notice, too, how the engine runs, if there is any tendency to " race," also if it will not " tick over " slowly. This may be due to worn valve guides or carburetter

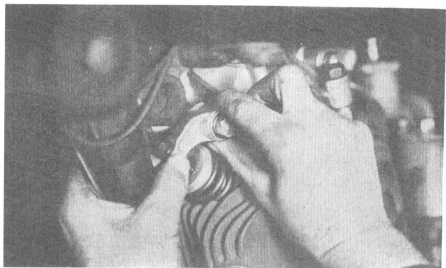

Fig. 4A. —A SPECIAL TEST FOR O.H.V. MACHINES.

See that the overhead valve rockers are not sloppy on their spindles.   The method of doing this is clearly shown in the picture above.

slides—these may be checked later.

Examine Contact Breaker

Remove the contact-breaker cover and look for any sparking at the contact points. This causes rapid burning away of the points, and will lead to trouble later on, although the machine may continue to function until the points are completely burnt away.

Now test for Compression

The oil by this time will have thoroughly thinned down, so the engine may be shut off and the compression tested. Open the throttle and air lever and stand on the kick-starter. Appreciable resistance should be felt when the engine goes over the compression

Fig. 4B.—TESTING THE VALVE AND TAPPET GUIDES.

To find out if the valve or tappet guides are worn, turn the engine on to the compression stroke (to free the tappets), then try to push the valve stem or tappet from side to side as shown above.

Fig. 5.—TESTING THE MAIN BEARINGS.
Grasp the sprocket boss as shown, and try to lift it up and down. This is a
simple but effective test for worn bearings.

stroke. If this is not the case, the piston and/or rings may be worn,
valve seatings may be leaking, or the cylinder may be scored.

Testing a Twin-cylinder Machine for Compression

In the case of a twin-cylindered engine, remove one sparking plug and
test the other cylinder for compression in the same manner.

Any Cracks in Cylinder ?

Examine the cylinder, as far as possible, for cracks. After the engine
has been running, it is usually possible to detect signs of oil creeping
through any cracks or blowholes. In this respect pay particular attention to the region of the valve caps in a side-valve cylinder.

Now look at Valve and Tappet Guides

Now test the valve and tappet guides. Rotate the engine until it is
on the compression stroke, i.e. both tappets clear of the valves or rockers
in an o.h.v. model. Endeavour to push the valve stem or tappet from
side to side. If there is any play it may be necessary to replace tappets,
valves and guides. In the case of an o.h.v. engine see that the rockers
are not sloppy on the bearing spindles. (See Figs. 4A and 4B.)

The Engine Sprocket

Remove the chaincases and chains, and examine the engine sprocket,
the teeth of which often become "hooked" when used with stretched chains.

The Main Bearings

The main bearings may now be tested by grasping the sprocket boss firmly with both hands, an effort being made to lift this up and down (see Fig. 5). The amount of movement will indicate the amount of wear on the main bearings. Do not, however, confuse this with endplay—a certain amount up to $\frac{1}{8}$ inch is usually allowed, although anything above this will have to be dealt with.

How to detect Play in Con-rod Bearings without Dismantling

It is possible in some cases to detect wear on big- or small-end bearings by rotating the sprocket until compression is felt, then rocking the sprocket backward and forward.

Carburetter

This may be checked by unscrewing the knurled ring securing the controls and slides, and removing the latter completely, when any wear will be detected (see Fig. 6).

Magneto

Only minor tests can be carried out on the magneto; these principally refer to the contact points. These should be examined for pitting and unevenness, thus confirming any sparking at the points noticed when the engine was running. The armature bearings can be tested to a limited extent in a similar manner to that suggested for the engine

Fig. 6.—A Possible Cause of Bad Starting.

This picture gives a good idea of where to look for wear on throttle slides. It will be noted that the outer slide groove which registers with a guide in the carburetter body is very badly worn and is considerably out of parallel. This will have the effect of making the control erratic.

main bearings. Note if the high-tension lead is perished or the carbon brush holder cracked.

Chains—Two Tests for Wear

A badly worn chain causes noise, excessive wear to the sprocket teeth and is impossible to adjust. Test the chains for stretch by alternately pulling and pushing whilst holding the ends (see Figs. 8A and 8B). Also note if any rollers are missing. Before testing, a chain should be thoroughly cleansed of all grit and grease by scrubbing in a paraffin bath. It is extremely doubtful if a prospective purchaser would be able to carry out a test of this description, in which case he should note if the chains fit the sprockets snugly, and to check this should endeavour to pull the chain

Fig. 7.—Testing the Magneto Bearings.
Remove the contact-breaker cover and grasp the end of the armature spindle between finger and thumb as shown. Excessive play in the bearings will easily be detected, as in the case of the main bearing (Fig. 5).

from the sprocket or chain wheel (see Fig. 9). If this is possible the chain is probably stretched.

Gearbox and Clutch

Check the clutch assembly for play in the gearbox main bearing as directed for the engine, by endeavouring to lift this up and down. It is very useful to note too if the oil is being thrown out of the gearbox. This can very often be detected on the rear tyre, and whilst this may be due to a damaged oil-retaining washer, it may also be due to a worn bush. Examine for endplay by pulling and pushing the clutch body towards

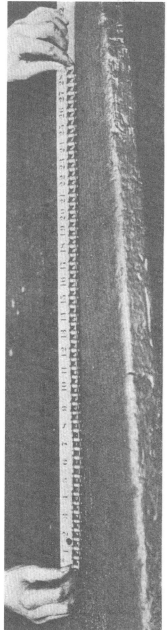

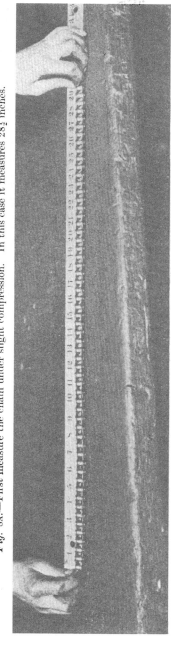

Fig. 8A.—First measure the chain under slight compression. In this case it measures 28½ inches.

Fig. 8B.—Then pull the chain out as far as it will go, and note the new measurement. In this case 29½ inches.

A SEARCHING TEST FOR DRIVING CHAINS.

If you wish to find out whether a driving chain has worn to a considerable extent, first remove the chain from the machine, clean it thoroughly in paraffin, and then lay it flat on a table or bench. Now measure it as shown in Fig. 8A above, under slight compression. Then stretch the chain to its limit and note the new measurement (Fig. 8B). The difference should not exceed ¼ inch. In the picture above the difference is 1 inch—a bad case. If a chain in this condition is continued in use, rapid wear on the sprocket and chain-wheel teeth is sure to take place. (These may be kept for use when the transmission article is dealt with.)

Fig. 9.—A ROUGH-AND-READY TEST FOR CHAIN WEAR.

If when the chain is pulled in this manner a space can be seen between the chain and chain wheel, this denotes either a stretched chain or badly worn teeth on wheel.

the gearbox ; anything over $\frac{1}{8}$ inch denotes wear on the thrust bearing. With the gearbox lever in neutral, withdraw the clutch, and note if the clutch plates revolve freely when the kick-starter is operated, also engage the clutch and see that this holds when standing on the kick-starter against the compression of the engine. Examine the gear operating lever for wear between the knuckles or yokes and the pins.

Wheels

Check the rims for truth by spinning the wheel and holding a pointer as near the rim as possible, checking any error as the wheel revolves (see Fig. 10). Make sure the spokes are tight and that all are intact ; these usually break at the hub flanges. Test the wheel bearings by attempting to rock the wheel sideways in the forks. There should be no play with ball bearings, but with roller bearings a certain amount of play is always allowed. The wheel should revolve quite freely and smoothly ; any grating, clicking or roughness denotes worn or pitted bearings.

General Alignment

If the wheels are not badly buckled the alignment of the machine should be checked. A ready method is by sighting along the lower part of the wheels some distance from the machine ; needless to say, one should be directly behind the other. A surer method, however, is to apply a straight-edged board or a length of tightly stretched string along the wheels as high up as possible from the wheel base (see Fig. 11). If the wheels are in correct alignment the board or string should make contact at four points. Should this not be the case check the rear-wheel chain adjusters. If these are level then the frame or forks are out of truth. (Further tests will be given when these parts are dealt with in later articles.)

Testing the Front Forks and Steering Head — a Warning

Raise the front of the machine off the ground by supporting the crankcase on a box or can. Tighten the steering damper to prevent the forks swinging. Determine the amount of play in the fork spindles and links,

Fig. 10.—TESTING THE WHEEL RIM FOR TRUTH.
Hold a pencil or piece of chalk near the rim, and spin the wheel as shown.

when the front assembly is lifted by the mudguard or lower part of the fork blades (see Fig. 12). If there is much up-and-down play it is well to remove the links and examine the fork spindles and the housings. The reader should also beware of forks where the spindles are rusted solid ;

it is very often an expensive matter to remove these. The support may now be removed and the machine lowered to the ground. The head races may now be tested. Stand astride the machine, slacken off the steering damper (if top type is fitted disconnect this altogether), pull upwards on the handlebars and note any play between the races. Swing the handlebars from side to side ; if the steering is jerky and tight in places, the head races are pitted and should be renewed. If a click is noticed, this may be due to broken balls or a slack fork link.

Fig. 11.—A TEST FOR WHEEL ALIGNMENT.

Stretch a string across the two wheels as shown. If the wheels are in correct alignment the string will make contact *at two points on the rim of each wheel.* In the picture the wheels are not in alignment.

SOME TESTS FOR THE BRAKES, WITH THE MACHINE STATIONARY

Worn Linings

The brakes are better tested on the road ; there are, however, a few notes that may be taken into consideration. The brake should be applied " hard " and the position of the brake cam lever noted. This should not be at more than right angles to the operating rod or cable (see Figs. 13 and 14). Should the angle be greater, then it is possible that the drum and/or the linings will shortly require renewing.

Is the Brake Release Good ?

It should also be noticed if there is any tendency for the brakes to stick " on." Whilst this may be due to rusty or stiff controls, it may also be due to the brake cam going over " dead centre," also indicating worn drum and linings.

Is the Brake Drum True ?

Now spin the wheel and gently apply the brake ; if the pedal or hand lever tends to move up and down, most likely the drum is out of truth.

Fig. 12.—EXAMINING THE FORKS.

Look for excessive play in the links and in the fork spindles. Note that for this test the front of the machine is supported clear of the ground.

This will cause the brake to be fierce in action.   Should the rear wheel be too stiff to spin, the engine may be started.   With the machine on the stand and the gear engaged, the pedal can be progressively applied and the effect noted.

Some Useful Notes on Chain Wheels

Make sure the chain wheel is tight on the hub ; in the case of Enfield type cush hubs, too much back and forward movement denotes worn rubber shock absorbers.   In types with detachable rear wheels examine for independent movement between the chain wheel and the wheel hub ; this indicates worn splines, dogs or pegs according to the type of fixing.

The Electrical Equipment

Examine the battery, paying particular attention to the lugs and connecting bridges.   See these are firm and the leads secured to the lugs. Remove the vent plugs and examine the plates for " sulphation," a greenish white deposit ; note too if the plates are covered with acid. Switch on the large headlamp bulb for a time and mark any reduction in volume of light.   Start the engine, and note by the ammeter whether the dynamo is charging.

Detailed tests and remedies for any faults discovered will be given in a later article.   The present notes are intended to assist the owner or purchaser to make a rapid inspection without missing any vital points.

General Notes—Tubes, Petrol Tank, Control Cables

Look over frame, rear stays and fork tubes for dents : these seriously weaken the structure ; also for cracked tubes, particularly examine behind the lugs.   Look into the petrol tank for signs of rust, also underneath the bottom for leaks, principally at the tap boss and where the frame bolts are screwed into the tank.   Regard any blobs of solder with suspicion. Where the oil tank is incorporated with the petrol tank examine the contents and make sure these are not leaking into each other.   Control cables should be examined for frayed wires or any stiffness in action. This may be due to trapped casings ; also examine for any slackness in the inner wire or play in the twist grip control.   Note if the nuts and screw heads have been mutilated.

Examining the Sidecar

Examine the chassis frame for general alignment and the tubes for fractures.   Look for possible wear in the spring eyes and shackles where these are fitted.   Check sidecar wheel bearings as previously directed. Examine the connecting tubes and lugs.   Make sure the clips are the correct size for the tubes.   Pay attention to fixing bolts where the body is attached to the bearer bars.

Fig. 13.—A Sign of a Badly Worn Brake.
Note the angle between the brake lever and the rod when the brake is applied.

Fig. 14.—Brake in Good Condition.
This shows the correct angle between the lever and rod with the brake applied.

15

RUNNING TESTS

If you are not allowed a Road Test

In this case the machine must be tested as far as possible on the stand. Start the engine and engage each gear in turn. Apply the brake gradually and open the throttle at the same time. As the load of the brake increases on the engine it will be possible to note any undue noise.

A harsh grinding sound would confirm a worn primary chain, whilst a pitted ballrace would give rather *a high-pitched whir*, rising and falling according to the engine speed. *A dull knock*, increasing as the load is applied, would rather indicate a worn connecting-rod bearing.

Testing the Gears, Clutch and Brake

The engine may be given full throttle for a moment in each gear and almost " stalled " by the brake. This will test each gear for any tendency to jump out of mesh and incidentally the clutch and brake.

If it is found that it is impossible to stall the engine, but that it rather accelerates, either the clutch is slipping or the brake is weak.

Piston Wear

Allow the engine to " tick over," and if on momentarily opening the throttle a sharp metallic tapping is noticed, it would rather point to piston slap due to a worn piston or cylinder bore. Retard the ignition, and if the slap disappears this would not be considered serious.

TESTS ON THE ROAD

Does the Engine accelerate well ?

The foregoing points may also be noticed if it is possible to take the machine on the road. In addition, " pick up " and acceleration can be gauged. Any tendency to " pink " may indicate, amongst other things, a badly carbonised engine.

The Steering, the Gears and the Clutch

With a machine that is steering correctly it should be possible to ride " hands off " at any speed over 15 miles per hour. Do not, however, demonstrate these qualities to a policeman, he may not appreciate them.

Note the gear and clutch operation. This should be quiet and the clutch engagement progressive and smooth. Give the engine full throttle in lower gears to test gear meshing.

After the Road Test

On return examine the engine for oil leaks, etc. It should be possible now to form some idea of the extent of the repairs and any spare parts that will be necessary. The manufacturers' spare parts list will enable you to assess the amount that may have to be spent to put the machine in good repair.

HOW TO USE AN ENGINE TIMING DISK

By J. Earney, M.I.M.T.

Fig. 1.—Timing a Magneto.

This shows an engine timing disk in use for checking the setting of a magneto. The ignition lever has, of course, been set at full advance, and the timing disk has been turned to the makers' correct setting of 35° before top dead centre on the compression stroke. It will be seen that the points of the contact breaker are just beginning to open.

THE use of a timing disk will enable you to obtain a greater degree of accuracy than by the measurement of the piston travel. The disk is fitted to the mainshaft on the sprocket side of the engine. On some models it is possible to fit this on the shaft between the sprocket and the nut securing it. On others, where the nut is recessed in the cush-drive assembly, it will be necessary to remove this complete and fit the timer up to the shoulder on the shaft. Measure the diameter of the shaft and drill out the centre of the disk accordingly : you will note there are circles already drawn to aid you. It is advisable to cut the hole slightly under size, this will allow the shaft to cut a thread in the soft millboard and so steady the disk whilst the readings are being taken.

Fig. 2.—First check the Tappet or Rocker Clearances.

The first thing to do when retiming the valves or checking the timing is to see that the tappet clearances are correct. Many makers specify the correct clearances, but a good average working figure is ·002 inch. The picture shows a feeler gauge being used to adjust the rocker clearance on an overhead valve type of engine.

When rotating the engine, screw the nut on the shaft and use a spanner for the necessary leverage.

Valve Timing

First check the clearances of the tappets or rockers to say ·002. These pinions may be in any position, but make quite sure the cams have not started to lift. Now rotate the engine until the piston is at the top of the stroke, commonly referred to as top dead centre (T.D.C.). This can be ascertained by inserting a rule or timing stick through the sparking-plug hole. Then set the timing approximately by inserting the pinions so that the cams are " on the rock," that is, with the inlet valve just opening and the exhaust just closing. The engine will probably function with this setting, but not so efficiently as with the manufacturer's recommended setting.

To check this, therefore, fit the timer to the shaft, together with the nut. Now fit a short length of wire or a strip of tin under one of the cylinder or crankcase nuts to act as a pointer. Make sure the piston is at T.D.C., then set the pointer at 0—T.D.C. Confirm these relative positions by turning the engine backward and forward, say ½ inch down the stroke, and note the reading in degrees on the timer. If this is greater on one side, say 40° when the engine was turned in a forward direction and only 36° in a backward direction, then the pointer will have to be adjusted 2° forward, thus giving 38° each side.

To set the cams is now a comparatively simple operation. Supposing

Fig. 3.—PLACING THE TIMING DISK IN POSITION.

After checking the clearances of the tappets or rockers, remove one of the sparking plugs and insert a rule or timing stick through the sparking-plug hole. Fit the disk on the shaft, replacing the nut. Fit a short length of wire to one of the engine bolts to serve as a pointer. Now turn the engine to bring the piston to T.D.C., and set the disk so that the pointer reads T.D.C. on the disk.

Fig. 4.—CHECKING THE SETTING OF THE DISK.

To make sure that T.D.C. has been found correctly, turn the engine *forward* ½ inch down the stroke. Note the reading on the disk. In the case above the reading on the disk is 40°. Now refer to the next illustration.

Fig. 5.—Checking the Setting of the Disk.

Next turn the engine *backward* ½ inch down the stroke, and note the new reading. If both readings are the same the disk is set correctly. In the present case the first reading was 40° and the second reading is 36°, so the disk must be moved backward 2°. In practice it will be easier to move the pointer 2° forward. This serves the same purpose.

Fig. 6.—SETTING THE INLET VALVE OPENING.

This shows the setting for the inlet valve to open 20° before T.D.C.   Check as shown in Fig. 8.   To reset the timing remove the cover of the timing case, which is at the opposite side of the engine.   (See Fig. 7.)

Fig. 7.—SETTING THE INLET CAM PINION.

With the disk set as in Fig. 6 refit the inlet cam pinion as shown. The inlet cam is being fitted so that it is about to lift the push rod. In this particular engine the rod is spring loaded, and a screwdriver is used to take the load of the return spring.

the inlet valve should commence to open 20° before T.D.C. Then turn the engine backward to 20° on the timer, and refit the inlet cam pinion so that this is just about to lift on the cam. This may be checked in turn by watching the tappet adjustment (set to ·002) ; as the engine is just slightly rotated in a forward direction, the clearance should be immediately taken up. In an engine with a double-cam pinion this is all that is necessary, as the relative positions between the inlet and exhaust cams are fixed. Where a separate cam pinion is fitted to the exhaust, proceed to set this in the same way. Supposing again the exhaust valve is intended to open 55° before bottom dead centre (B.D.C.). Rotate the engine in a forward direction one complete revolution, and continue rotating until the point 55° before B.D.C. is reached at the pointer. The exhaust cam pinion can then be refitted and checked, as advised in the case of the inlet. *A series of Timing Charts, giving the makers' settings for all the popular motor-cycles, will be given later in this work.*

Fig. 8.—A Final Check.
With the cam pinion in position insert a feeler gauge underneath the rocker or tappet and move the engine shaft forward very slightly. If the setting is correct the gauge will be gripped immediately.
Note.—In many engines the inlet and exhaust cams are in one piece, so that when one is set the other is correct. If the exhaust cam is separate it can be set in the same manner as the inlet cam.

Magneto Timing

If so desired, the magneto can be timed in a similar manner. Rotate the engine until the 0—T.D.C. *on the compression stroke* registers with the pointer. Supposing the recommended timing is 35° advance, then turn the engine backward to the 35° mark and set the contact breaker accordingly (see Fig. 1).

(*Note.*—The timing of magnetos will be dealt with fully in a specia article.)

REPAIR NOTES ON LEVIS ENGINES

By W. S. BANNER (*of Butterfields, Ltd.*)

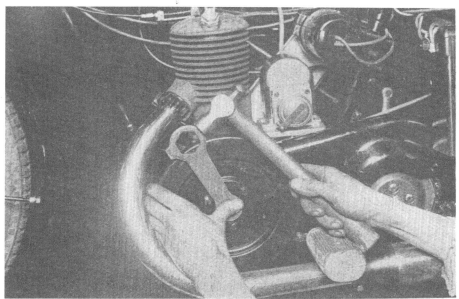

Fig. 1.—REMOVING THE FLYWHEEL—FIRST OPERATION.
Use a hammer and spanner as shown above to loosen the flywheel nut.

TWO-STROKE MODELS

WITH certain exceptions in the case of the " Six-Port " model, which is referred to on pages 33–8, the methods of dismantling all Levis two-stroke models are almost identical.

How to remove the Flywheel

The first operation is to remove the flywheel, which operation should be performed in the following manner. After unscrewing the flywheel nut (ordinary right-hand thread), the end of the crankshaft should be given one or two sharp square blows with a fairly heavy hammer. At the same time, hold the flywheel firmly with one hand and pull away from the engine. At the first or second blow, the flywheel should come

Fig. 2.—Removing the Flywheel—Second Operation.
Tap the end of the shaft with a hammer, hold the flywheel firmly with one hand, and pull away from engine.

Fig. 3.—Replacing the Flywheel.
In this case the final tightening of the flywheel nut should be carried out as above, using the spanner and hammer.

away, and, if the blows are square and decided, no damage will be done to the threads on the end of the crankshaft, as the end of the shaft is toughened.

Dealing with Obstinate Cases

The flywheel should come off, however obstinate, if one person holds the flywheel firmly by its rim, at the same time pulling away from the engine, whilst a second person uses the hammer on the end of the crankshaft as mentioned above. It should be carefully noted that a hammer of less than 1½ lb. is quite useless for this job.

No key is used to secure the flywheel to the shaft, the fixing relying solely upon the taper. This applies to all Levis two-stroke models, with the exception of a comparatively small number of machines turned out in pre-war days. These were fitted with keys, but it is recommended that the use of the key be discontinued, as it has no holding value. Quite obviously such a small key cannot possibly be expected to hold a flywheel of such weight and diameter.

If a Flywheel works Loose—a Warning

It is important to note that, in the case of trouble with the flywheel coming loose upon the taper, it is not of the slightest use to endeavour to secure it with the aid of a key. If this is attempted, all that will happen, when the engine is started up, is that the flywheel will shear the key, thus irreparably damaging both the taper of the crankshaft and the bore of the flywheel. In this case, the only remedy is new parts.

Removing the Cylinder

The removal of the cylinder does not present any difficulty, and in the case of all Levis models, the cylinder can be removed without taking the engine out of the frame. In the case, however, of those models where the tank is mounted on two detachable tubes, it is advisable to remove the tank first, as by doing this the job is made very much more easy and convenient. The time saved more than compensates for the time taken to remove and replace the tank, and moreover, there is far less danger of damaging the piston or straining the connecting rod than when trying to work in a confined space. In the case of recent models with saddle tank, the frame has a second rail upon which the tank is mounted, and in this case there is no advantage in removing the tank first.

An Important Precaution

When removing the cylinder, it is very advisable to stuff the inside of the piston with rag before the cylinder actually comes away. Otherwise the heavy deflector head of the piston will cause the skirt to come sharply in contact with the connecting rod immediately the cylinder is removed, and which is quite likely to crack the piston.

About Gudgeon Pins

There are broadly two different types of gudgeon pin in use in Levis two-stroke engines : firstly, a taper gudgeon pin of $\frac{7}{16}$-inch diameter ; and secondly, a parallel gudgeon pin of $\frac{1}{2}$-inch diameter, the latter type being fitted to the recent models. The early $\frac{7}{16}$-inch taper gudgeon pins rely entirely upon the taper to secure them in the piston bosses, in which case, of course, the gudgeon pin is a rather tight fit in the piston. In the case of these, the utmost care must be used in dismantling to avoid distorting or breaking the piston. The gudgeon pin should be driven out with a hammer and a brass punch, whilst the piston is well supported on the other side. These taper gudgeon pins drive out towards the flywheel.

Fig. 4.—DEALING WITH AN AWKWARD NUT.
The cylinder base nut behind the magneto chain cover must be removed as shown above. Note that two thin spanners are required for this purpose.

In the case of the $\frac{7}{16}$-inch taper gudgeon pins which have circlips in the piston bosses, these are not so tight, and removal is therefore not fraught with much difficulty or risk of damage. Wherever a $\frac{1}{2}$-inch gudgeon pin is fitted, it will be found to be parallel and a comparatively loose fit, so that it may be pushed out either way after, of course, the circlips have been removed.

Prising Crankcase Apart

After the piston has been taken off and the crankcase bolts removed, the crankcase halves should be carefully prised asunder. Use the handle of a hammer or a piece of wood between the two halves, or tap one of the cylinder base studs lightly with it. As crankcase compression is used in a two-stroke, care should be used to prevent damage to the faces of the crankcase halves whilst they are dismantled.

An Important Note for dismantling the Big End

The taking down of the big end will be obvious, but it should be noted that each time this operation is performed, new big-end pins will be required. They are not intended to be used more than once, and new pins should be obtained before starting upon the job. The big-end bearing is plain and of phosphor bronze, being made in two halves. Shims are used to fill in the gap of the sawcut which has divided the bearing. After the big end has been dismantled, the engine will have been resolved into its component parts.

Examine Piston for Wear—a Cause of "Two-stroke Rattle"

When decarbonising, it is highly important to clean off every trace of carbon from the sides of the deflector head of the piston and from the cylinder walls inside near the top. Any sign of excessive wear or binding of the piston, especially the one side at the top and the opposite side at the bottom, indicates that the alignment of the connecting rod has suffered, and this should have the careful attention of a capable and experienced engine fitter, or the necessary engine parts returned to the makers for attention. These two items are sometimes responsible for the elusive "two-stroke rattle" which has given rise to so many discussions amongst motor-cyclists.

Re-erecting—the Big End

Let us now deal with the process of re-erecting. In assembling the big end and refitting same to the one-piece crankshaft, the two new big-end pins should be screwed up tight with a tubular spanner, and after they are home, split the threaded ends and splay same open slightly like a split pin. Also, do not forget to file off the corners

Fig. 5.—METHOD OF REMOVING THE CYLINDER.

Observe that the inside of the piston is stuffed with rag to prevent it from becoming damaged by contact with the connecting rod when the cylinder is actually lifted off.

of the hexagon heads of the big-end pins, as unless this is done there is not enough clearance in the crankcase.

If it is necessary for a new big-end bearing to be fitted, it should be noticed that this has to be pegged and scraped in the usual way. Slight play can be taken up by filling the shims previously referred to. These should be secured on a board with short tacks or nails, the latter being driven almost home so as not to project above the surface of the shim. The shims should then be filed until the play has been taken up.

Cleaning out Crankcase and Oilways

Before refitting the crankshaft in the crankcase, take the opportunity of swilling this out thoroughly in paraffin, so that the oilways may have a good clean. The crankshaft is drilled as part of the Levis lubrication system. The oilways in the crankcase bearings should also be similarly swilled.

Worn Main Bearings

The main bearings should be examined for play, and if this is only slight, renewal should not be necessary. Do not worry too much about crankcase compression as regards the bearings, as it has been proved time and again that the bearings invariably require renewal for mechanical reasons

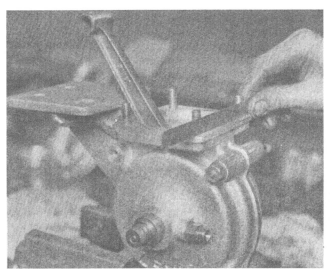

Fig. 6.—An Important Test when reassembling a Levis Crankcase.

Lay a straightedge across the two halves to make sure that they are in line. A perfect joint is of first importance, because of the use of the crank chamber for compression.

long before the loss of compression is sufficient to have any effect upon the efficiency or performance of the engine. If the main bearings are badly worn and really require renewal, it is advisable to return the crankcase to the makers to have this done, as few garages and still fewer owners are likely to have a line reamer such as is necessary to ensure that the main bearings are in alignment. With an ordinary reamer, it is quite possible for the bearings to be reamered individually, and each one apparently quite all right in its own half of the case, but all this is quite useless if by any chance the bearings should not be in alignment when the crankcase is bolted up. If it is impossible for the crankcase to be returned for this work to be done by the makers, then the utmost care should be taken to get everything as good as possible, and after the crankcase has been bolted up with the crankshaft in place, turn the crankshaft round to make quite sure that it revolves freely when turned with the finger and thumb.

Fitting New Little-end Bush

With regard to the little-end bush, should this require renewal and a replacement part has been obtained from the makers, it will be found to be oversize. This is necessary, as a standard new bush would be slack in the hole in the top end of the connecting rod after the original bearing has been removed, as the hole is necessarily slightly enlarged in so doing. Before fitting, therefore, the bush should be turned to the correct size outside. As regards the inside of the bearing, if this is to fit a taper gudgeon pin, then a taper reamer is necessary in order to ensure a nice fit. When the gudgeon pin has been replaced, do not forget to fit two new circlips unless the gudgeon pin is of a very early type where circlips were not fitted.

Do not forget that when any or all of the three phosphor-bronze bushes are replaced, the new bush or bushes must be drilled where requisite with the necessary oil holes *after the bush has been fitted in place*.

Is Sideplay in Bearings Important ?

No jointing washer is required between the two halves of the crank-case, but these should be scrupulously clean, and it is a good plan to paint the edges of the joint with goldsize before reassembling. One point that owners often raise is with regard to sideplay in the bearings, and it may be here stated definitely that sideplay alone is absolutely immaterial. In fact, a certain amount of sideplay is necessary, and unless there is an appreciable up-and-down play the bearings do not require renewal.

Refitting Cylinder

When the crankcase has been bolted together and before finally tightening everything up, put a straightedge across the top of the crankcase to ensure that this is absolutely level. Otherwise when you come to screw down the cylinder, there is a possibility of breaking it unless it beds down perfectly evenly on to the flat top of the crankcase.

The usual paper washer is required between the cylinder and the crankcase, and after making one for this purpose, *do not forget to cut out a hole to correspond with the transfer port !* The usual washer is also required between the exhaust port and the exhaust pipe in cases where the exhaust pipe is attached to the cylinder by means of either two or four pins. Obviously, in the case of those engines where the exhaust pipe is merely a push-in fit in the lug, no washer is required. In the case of the induction port (if the carburetter lug has been removed) no washer is required at this point ; the surfaces should be absolutely clean and treated with goldsize before reassembling.

Fig. 7.—Not a Job for the Amateur.

If the main bearings have to be renewed, it is best to return the crankcase to the makers. The process of reamering out the bearings can only be done by using the special line reamer shown above.

See if Valve is Gastight

Before refitting the release valve in the top of the cylinder head, it is as well to just inspect this and see that it is gastight. As the little valve is not exposed to the flame as regards the seating, except on very rare occasions, it does not require very frequent attention, but if it is pitted or obviously not making a gastight joint, it should be ground in in the usual way. If the little spring has lost its tension, it should be replaced.

Care in replacing Flywheel

When replacing the flywheel great care should be taken that both the end of the crankshaft and the hole in the flywheel are perfectly clean and free from grease or grit. The illustration on page 26 shows the manner in which the flywheel nut should be finally tightened. It is not sufficient to merely pull up this nut as tight as possible with a spanner by hand. The special spanner supplied by the makers must be used, and the nut " jarred " up deadtight by hammering the end of the spanner as far as it will go. Take particular care that there is sufficient thread on the end of the crankshaft remaining below the face of the flywheel

Fig. 8.—TESTING THE BEARINGS.
The crankshaft should be capable of being easily rotated by means of the finger and thumb.

boss to allow the nut to force the wheel deadtight upon the taper without fouling the last thread. A movable spanner is not sufficiently strong for this job.

FOUR-STROKING—ITS CAUSE AND REMEDY

Four-stroking (unless caused by overoiling) is due to an excessively rich mixture, and if the float level is correct (easily checked by a reference to the maker's booklet), the remedy is to fit a smaller jet. The best way is to get several smaller jets and try them one by one, each smaller than the preceding one, till the engine two-strokes to your satisfaction. It must be remembered that the engine will two-stroke at walking pace, but to obtain this means using a smaller jet than is really advisable, as a certain amount of power at larger throttle openings would thereby be sacrificed. A setting which is a compromise to suit one's own taste can usually be obtained, and it is best to tolerate a little four-stroking downhill or at very low speeds.

THE " SIX-PORT " TWO-STROKE MODELS

The " Six-Port " engine differs from other Levis two-strokes in three main respects :

(1) It is the only Levis two-stroke engine with twin exhaust pipes.

3

Fig. 9A.—TIMING THE MAGNETO—FIRST OPERATION.

This shows the method of timing the magneto in the case of two-stroke models with the plug in the side of the cylinder. Operation 1.—Get the piston on top dead centre and put a chalk mark on the flywheel, together with one on the cylinder so that both marks are in line as shown above.

(2) It is the only Levis two-stroke engine wherein an aluminium alloy piston is employed ; and

(3) It is the only two-stroke model with a detachable head.

Points to Note when Decarbonising

As regards the general dismantling of the engine, this should be carried out on the same lines as the other two-stroke models, but in dismantling the cylinder, the head should be first removed. Owing to the superior performance of the " Six-Port " engine, it naturally requires more care and attention to keep it in tune than the ordinary models. Obviously, for the purpose of decarbonising only, it is not necessary to remove the cylinder barrel, as decarbonising can be done when the head has been taken off, but it is very advisable, whenever decarbonising is required, to take an opportunity to inspect the rings so that these may be freed, if they show a tendency

to stick, or re-
placed if ob-
viously worn.

Do not re-
move the trans-
fer passage
cover : it should
never be neces-
sary to remove
this. There is
no object in
breaking a good
joint, but if this
should be done
inadvertently,
note that a
washer is re-
quired between
the cover and the
cylinder barrel.

Removing Car-
bon from Piston

Great care
should be exer-
cised in remov-
ing carbon from
the piston of the
" Six-Port " en-
gine, as the
aluminium alloy
is very soft, and
could be cut with
a knife. Particu-
lar care is neces-
sary in cleaning
the ring slots so
as not to damage
them in any way.

Fig. 9B.—TIMING THE MAGNETO—SECOND OPERATION.
Place a second chalk mark on the cylinder where shown, and
turn the flywheel back until the chalk mark on it is in line with
the second chalk mark on the cylinder. The contact points should
just be breaking with ignition lever set at full retard.

How to wreck an Engine

When replacing the piston, be careful not to put it on back to front, as
owing to the shaped combustion head the engine will be wrecked if an
attempt is made to even turn it round with the kick-starter. The gentle
slope of the deflector head is towards the exhaust ports. In any two-stroke

3*

model, care should be taken that the piston is put on the right way, but in the case of the other models nothing more serious than a loss of power will be experienced. With the " Six-Port," there is the above real danger, and therefore great care should be exercised not to make this mistake.

There is a plain copper washer between the head and the barrel, and this should be replaced if damaged. When fitting this copper washer, be careful to put it on with the hole in register with the release valve passage to the exhaust manifold. Also see that the passage in question is clear.

MAGNETO TIMING INSTRUCTIONS

Engines with the Sparking Plug in the Rear of the Cylinder

If with Variable Ignition.—Turn the flywheel until the piston is dead on top centre. This position can be seen by removing the plug and looking in through the hole. Place the " Advance " lever in " Fully Retarded " position, when the magneto points should just have broken.

Fig. 10.—Removing the Head of the Levis " Six-Port " Model.

If with Fixed Ignition.—Turn the flywheel forward till piston reaches top of the stroke ; now turn flywheel backward until piston has descended $\frac{3}{16}$ to $\frac{5}{16}$ inch, according to the circumstances (for hilly country $\frac{3}{16}$ inch is recommended, whilst for a comparatively flat district $\frac{5}{16}$ inch may be used). The points should just be in the act of breaking.

Engines with the Sparking Plug in the Side of Cylinder Head

It must be carefully noted that this type of engine does not require, *and will not stand*, as much advance as the other models.

Fig. 11.—The Piston of the Levis " Six-Port " Model in Place.
Note that the gentle slope of the deflector head of the piston is towards the exhaust ports.

" Six-Port " Model

Get piston on top dead centre, and put a chalk mark on the flywheel. Then turn the flywheel back $1\frac{1}{4}$ inches. The points should be just breaking and the ignition lever fully retarded. This equals 2 mm. of advance with the ignition lever fully retarded or $7\frac{1}{2}$ mm. of advance with the ignition lever fully advanced. The ignition timing of the " Six-Port " engine is of vital importance, and it will be found that it will stand much earlier timing than previous Levis models to advantage.

If slow running is required with even two stroking down to exceedingly slow speeds, and high speed is not of consequence, then the magneto timing may be set much later. The most suitable slow timing is best arrived at by experiment to suit the rider's requirements.

THE O.H.V. FOUR-STROKE MODELS

As the Levis models " A," " A1," " A2," " B " and " B Special " are all similar in design, the following remarks may be taken to apply to all the o.h.v. four-stroke machines made by this firm.

Dismantling the Cylinder

In order to dismantle the cylinder, slacken off the exhaust nut or nuts with the special spanner provided ; it is not necessary to completely remove the exhaust pipes when decarbonising. In the case of models dated early 1930 or previously, the rocker-box lid is attached by five small set pins, and it is not necessary to remove the lid or other parts when dismantling. In the case of late 1930 and subsequent models, in which the rocker-box lid is attached by a spring or central bolt, it is essential to remove the rockers before the head can be

Fig. 12.—Dismantling the Cylinder Head of the Levis O.H.V. Four-stroke—
First Operation

After the rocker-box lid has been removed, and the rockers withdrawn, the nuts underneath the rockers must be removed with a tubular spanner as shown.

taken off, as there are two nuts underneath the rockers which have to be undone. Slacken off the bottom push-rod tube nut, and then the rocker box, together with the push-rod tube, may be lifted off completely by the tube. Be careful to disengage the two push rods out of the cup-ended tappets and the whole should come away. The push rods are marked "left" and "right" respectively, so that there is no need to take any steps to keep them separate.

Fig. 13.—SECOND OPERATION.

The rocker box and push-rod tube can then be taken off in the manner shown, the right hand disengaging the push rods out of the cup-ended tappets.

Fig. 14.—THIRD OPERATION.

Removing the cylinder head from the barrel

Fig. 15.—ADJUSTING THE MAGNETO CHAIN.

After the two nuts (one on each side) have been slackened, the magneto can slide on its platform until the chain is at the requisite tension.

Fig. 16.—METHOD OF REMOVING THE MAGNETO.

Observe that the magneto must be canted over towards the cylinder before it can be lifted off.

Procedure for Decarbonising

Undo the nuts that secure the detachable head to the cylinder, when same can be lifted off ; if necessary, a little gentle prising will help. It is not necessary to remove the cylinder barrel except for examination purposes, and then only at fairly lengthy intervals. Even if the barrel is being removed, it is recommended that the carbon be removed from the top of the piston whilst the cylinder barrel is in position, as this greatly simplifies the work.

Useful Valve Removal and Grinding Tools

On the end of each valve will be found a small hardened cap, and care should be taken that these

Fig. 16.—REMOVING THE TIMING COVER FROM THE CRANK-CASE.

This must be pulled away square, as shown, until the oil tube is free of the mainshaft.

caps are not lost whilst the parts are dismantled. The valve removal is simple and the method obvious, but

Fig. 17.—HOW TO RE-TIME THE VALVES CORRECTLY.

A flat is ground off one of the teeth of the small pinion, and this tooth should be meshed between two teeth which have been similarly treated on the large pinion.

a special removing tool, such as the Hickman, is necessary.   A little device to assist in valve grinding can be obtained from the makers very cheaply.

Engine being Completely Dismantled

If, for any reason, the engine is being completely dismantled, the following notes should be most carefully observed.   In order to remove the sprocket adapter from the mainshaft, always use a sprocket drawer. *Under no circumstances must the end of the shaft be hammered.*   The mainshafts are a push-in fit in the flywheels on both sides, and if a hammer is used the result will simply be to drive the shaft through the flywheel and probably cause considerable damage.   In any case, it will most certainly be a job for the makers.

Methods of parting the Crankcase

Fig. 18.—THE SPROCKET ASSEMBLY OF THE LEVIS O.H.V. FOUR-STROKE.

Items are shown in the correct order, i.e. driving sprocket, distance piece, dynamo sprocket and lock ring.

In the case of early 1931 and all previous models the mainshaft is mounted on a ball bearing on the timing gear side, and a roller bearing on the driving side. Later models have a roller bearing both sides.   In the case of the models with the ball bearing on the timing side, some little difficulty may be experienced in parting the crankcase, owing to the bearing being inclined to stick on the shaft as a result of congealed oil or the like.   Bear in mind that the mainshaft must never be hammered as mentioned above, and the parting of the crankcase will be easily accomplished if the case itself in the vicinity of the ball bearing is warmed up for a few moments with a blowlamp. In this case, the aluminium of the crankcase will expand, and thus release the ball bearing which is only pressed into same.   The bearing will then come away with the shaft.   It should be noted that this does not apply to later 1931 models having a roller bearing on each side.

Flywheels

It is really not advisable to separate the flywheels if this can possibly be avoided, as this is essentially a job for the works. The special steel nuts which secure the crankpin must be really tightened up deadtight after the flywheels have been taken apart, and in order to verify that the alignment of the flywheels has not suffered, this should be tested with a piece of ½-inch (dead to size) round steel bar, which will just pass through two holes in the flywheels if they are perfectly in line.

Gudgeon Pin

The gudgeon pin is parallel and kept in place by circlips. It may therefore be pushed in or out either way. If it is a trifle tight either to remove or replace, warming the piston will be found effective.

Reassembling

There is no difficulty about the reassembling, and the method will be obvious. See that the copper washer between the cylinder barrel and head is perfectly clean and also both faces. Screw up the head nuts gently, half a turn at a time.

Fig. 19.—TESTING THE FLYWHEELS FOR ALIGNMENT.
Use a piece of dead-to-size ½-inch bar. This should just pass through the two holes in the flywheels.

The advantage of the plain copper washer is that no further tightening of the head will be found necessary when the engine has been run, as usually occurs when a C. & A. washer is fitted. When replacing the rocker box and push-rod tube assembly,

Fig. 20.—A WORKSHOP TIP FOR WITHDRAWING THE BALLRACE.
Use a blowlamp as shown, to warm up the crankcase round about the ballrace.
The expansion of the metal will allow the race to be withdrawn easily.

first of all insert the two push rods in the tube, holding them there with the fingers of the right hand. Then place the parts as nearly as possible into position, carefully noting that the lower ends of the push rods fit into their respective cups on the top of the tappets. Then manipulate the rocker box into position.

Magneto Timing

The magneto timing for all Levis o.h.v. models is as follows : piston on top dead centre, ignition lever fully retarded, platinum points just broken.

Tappet Clearance

The tappet clearance should be infinitesimal, i.e. about ·002 inch when cold. The top rockers are fitted with adjustable ball ends and lock nuts to provide tappet adjustment. The adjustment is easily made with the engine in place in the frame by using the specially cranked screwdriver provided and a spanner.

Other details of Levis machines will be dealt with in their appropriate sections, e.g. the Oiling System under Lubrication, and the Gearbox and Clutch, Brakes and Cycle Parts under their respective headings.

DECARBONISING YOUR MOTOR-CYCLE ENGINE

WITH NOTES ON GRINDING IN THE VALVES

By Lieut.-Col. D. J. Smith, O.B.E., M.I.A.E., *Past President of the Institution of Automobile Engineers*

THE operations, decarbonising and valve grinding, are really maintenance operations rather than repairs, and must be carried out periodically if the engine is to give its best performance.

Does your Machine need Decarbonising ?

The symptoms of decarbonising being required are : (1) overheating on comparatively light loads ; (2) loss of liveliness in picking up and acceleration ; (3) pinking or knocking when accelerating ; (4) engine continuing to fire when ignition is switched off, due to some portion of the carbon deposit becoming incandescent and igniting the charge ; (5) loss of power.

How to tell when the Valves need Attention

The symptoms of valve trouble are : (1) loss of compression : if the starter pedal is pressed down slowly there will be little resistance and the charge can probably be heard rushing past the valves ; (2) loss of power ; (3) overheating ; (4) poor acceleration ; (5) difficulty in starting ; (6) rough and irregular running, especially at slow speeds ; (7) high consumption of petrol and lubricating oil.

To carry out either operation the head or cylinder must be removed, so that both operations are usually done together, even if one or the other could have waited some time longer.

Why Engines need Decarbonising

There is no definite time or mileage period for these operations, especially decarbonising, which can be influenced by many things. The use of an unsuitable lubricating oil or petrol, running on too rich mixture, a slack piston or worn piston rings, allowing too much oil to get past, will all affect the amount of carbon formed. An engine which has a large number of starts and stops in proportion to the mileage run will need decarbonising sooner and more frequently than one used for long non-stop runs.

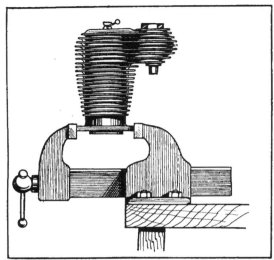

Fig. 1.—How to hold
Cylinder in Vice.

Cylinder held by flange in
vice to remove valve caps.
Before this is done the cylinder
mouth should be bridged.

A Useful Tip

Before removing the
cylinder from the en-
gine, take out the valve
caps, as if this is not
done it will be difficult
to remove them when
the cylinder is off unless
it can be held in a vice
as in Fig. 1.

This must be done
very carefully, as the
walls and flange of the
cylinder are thin, and
will not stand any degree
of crushing pressure as
applied by a vice.

To avoid cracking the Cylinder

If the cylinder has to
be held in a vice, it

When should a New Engine be Decarbonised ?

Some makers give
1,500 miles as the limit
of running a new engine
before decarbonising,
and double this distance
subsequently, but there
is really no rule on this
point. Whenever any of
the symptoms detailed
are present, the engine
should receive attention.
It will be assumed that
the engine in this case
is fitted with a solid
head cylinder and side-
by-side valves.

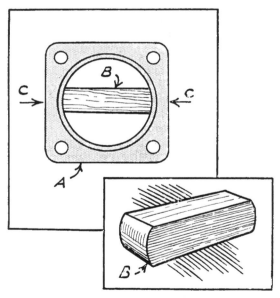

Fig. 2.—A Useful Tip.

Mouth of cylinder "bridged" by a block of hardwood to allow cylinder to be held in a vice by the
flange. A, Flange. B, Wood block rounded at ends
to fit bore tightly. Vice pressure must come in the
direction of arrows CC.

is advisable to bridge the mouth of the bore (Fig. 2). To do this, take a piece of hardwood—oak, ash, elm, mahogany, etc.—about 1 inch thick and 3 or 4 inches long. With a rasp or rough file round off the edges of a piece cut to a length just equal to the diameter of the bore until it is a tight fit in the cylinder. Tap this in lightly, and be careful to hold the cylinder so that the pressure comes in the direction the wood is placed.

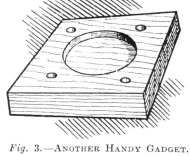

Fig. 3.—ANOTHER HANDY GADGET.

Block of hardwood about 1½ inches thick with four holes for cylinder flange bolts and recess cut out to take spigot of cylinder.

Another plan is to take a block of hardwood the same width as that of the cylinder over the flange and about 1½ inches thick. It can be 6 or 8 inches long. Mark a circle on this with a pair of dividers the same diameter as the spigot on the bottom of the cylinder (Fig. 3), and then with a wood chisel cut out the wood inside the circle deep enough to allow the spigot to drop in so that the face of the flange rests on the wood. Then drill four holes to corre-

Fig. 4.—BOLTS TO HOLD CYLINDER TO BLOCK OF WOOD IN FIG. 3.

spond with the bolt holes in the flange, and with four bolts bolt the cylinder on to the wood block. The bolts will cost about 1½d. each, and can be purchased at any ironmongers. Get the sort known as "round-square-hexagon" (Fig. 4), as the square will grip in the wood and prevent the bolts turning when doing up or undoing the nuts.

When mounted in this manner the cylinder can be held safely in the vice (Fig. 5). It is much more convenient to work on the cylinder if it can be held in this way. An air-cooled cylinder is a very difficult and delicate thing to handle otherwise, and ribs or fins are liable to be cracked or broken off if it is worked on while laying on a bench or table,

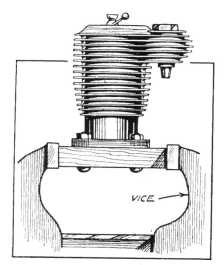

Fig. 5.—CYLINDER HELD BY BLOCK OF WOOD IN VICE.

If no vice is available, the wood block can be bolted to a bench or table.

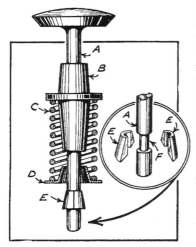

Fig. 6.—SHOWING SPRING COM-
PRESSED UP THE VALVE STEM,
AND SPRING WASHER D CLEAR
OF COTTER E, WHICH CAN NOW BE
REMOVED.

A, Valve. B, Guide. C, Spring.
D, Spring washer. E, Split coned
cotter. F, Recess on stem in
which cotter E fits.

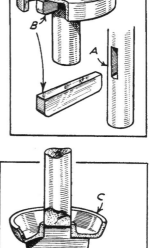

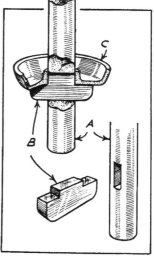

unless great care is used. To enable the valves to be removed the valve springs must be compressed up the valve stem until the valve spring washer is lifted free from the cotter (Fig. 6).

About Valve Cotters and their Removal

Various forms of valve cotters are used on motor-cycle valves, the commonest probably being that shown in Fig. 6, consisting of two halves of a coned steel sleeve fitting in a recess turned in the valve stem, the spring washer being coned to drop over the cotter and hold it into the groove in the valve stem. Other forms of cotters in use are shown in Figs. 7 and 8. Whatever type of cotter is fitted the procedure is the same: the spring must be compressed before it can be removed. There are many types of valve lifters—really spring compressors—on the market. One of the simplest and most useful for this type of cylinder is shown in Fig. 9. This is used as shown in Fig. 11, the forked end being put round the valve stem under the washer while the screw on the top is screwed down on to the head of the valve (Fig. 11), and this compresses the spring up the stem. The cotter will now be free (Fig. 6), and can be removed.

Fig. 7.—TWO TYPES OF VALVE COTTERS.

In (1) the valve spring washer has a round edge which drops over the cotter, preventing it coming out. In (2) the cotter has a raised centre part, over which the spring washer drops, preventing the cotter from moving.

AA, Valve stems. BB, Cotters. CC, Valve spring washers.

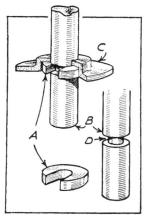

Fig. 8.—ANOTHER TYPE OF VALVE COTTER.

The cotter is slipped over the notch D in the valve stem B, and the recess in the spring washer C slips over it and prevents it coming out.

A, Cotter. B, Valve stem. C, Spring washer. D, Cotter notch.

If it is the split-cone type it may be tight on the stem, and if so, a thin tool, such as a small screwdriver forced into the joint (Fig. 6) will open the two halves and allow them to be removed. Cotters of types shown in Fig. 7 may be a tight fit in the slot and sometimes the edges get slightly burred up by the pressure of the washer, making them too wide to draw through the slot in the stem. If this is so, file the top edges of the cotter gently with a small smooth file (Fig. 12), and then draw out the cotter with a pair of pliers. Now remove the valve lifter, and, lifting the stem of the valve, slip off the spring washer and spring.

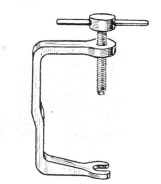

Fig. 9.—VALVE SPRING COMPRESSOR.

Forked end is put round valve stem under spring washer, and the screw is screwed down against the valve head.

Removing the Valves

When the cotter is removed and the lifter is taken away the valve washer may be forced down on to the tappet screw and be hard to remove. If so, pull the valve right out of the cylinder, and

LEVER "A" ENGAGES IN NOTCHES.

BY DEPRESSING LEVER, VALVE SPRING IS COMPRESSED.

COTTER MAY BE REMOVED WHEN SPRING IS COMPRESSED.

Fig. 10.—TERRY'S UNIVERSAL VALVE SPRING LIFTER.
This fits any engine. Self-sustaining, the lever A is held by notches on the long arm.

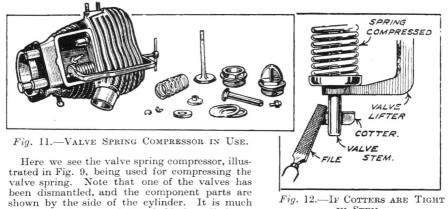

Fig. 11.—Valve Spring Compressor in Use.

Here we see the valve spring compressor, illustrated in Fig. 9, being used for compressing the valve spring. Note that one of the valves has been dismantled, and the component parts are shown by the side of the cylinder. It is much safer and more convenient to hold the cylinder as in Fig. 5 to carry out this work. It will be seen, on referring to the latter figure, that the cylinder should first be bolted to a block of wood.

Fig. 12.—If Cotters are Tight in Stem.

File top edges with a fine file to remove any burrs, and they can then be drawn out.

the spring and washer can then be slightly lifted and pulled out (Fig. 13).

A Note on Exhaust Valves

Note, the exhaust valve stem sometimes gets coated with carbonised oil under the bottom of the guide inside the spring, making it too tight to pass through the guide until this is removed. Do not try to force the stem up if this is so, as it will probably be bent in the attempt. Lift it as far as it will go by a little effort, and then, having taken off the spring washer by slightly compressing the spring, work the spring out coil by coil between the tappet and the bottom of the valve stem. For this purpose see that the valve tappet is at the bottom position; it will give more room.

Be Careful to mark the Valves

When the spring is off, drop the valve again on to its seat, and by means of a scraper, such as Fig. 14, made by grinding the end of a small file on the grindstone or emery wheel or an old wood chisel will do, scrape off the carbon. Do not use a file, or it will scratch the stem and lead to more deposit, the scratches forming a " key." Keep the valves separate; in some makes the exhaust valve differs in the shape of head, but in most cases a special metal is used for the exhaust valve, as this has to withstand a

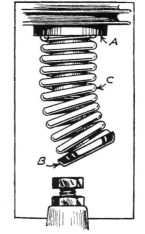

Fig. 13.—When Valves are removed without removing Cylinder.

The valve spring can be got off by forcing it sideways and drawing it off guide. A, Valve guide. B, Spring washer. C, Spring.

terrific heat.   If there is no distinguishing mark or shape, mark one valve by tying a piece of string on the cotter hole or a file notch on the stem *below* the cotter hole or slot. Even if the valves are the same in shape and metal, it is still not advisable to change them, as the inlet

Fig. 14.—An easily made Scraper.

A small triangular file or an old worn-out saw file will do, ground at point to form a scraper. Ground part shown plain XX.

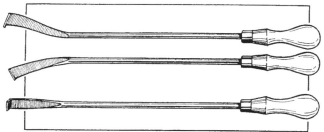

Fig. 15.—Set of Three Scrapers designed to get into all Parts of Cylinder Heads and Valve Ports.

valve, if used for the exhaust, would probably go out of shape slightly and leak when first exposed to the hot gases, needing another grinding in when the engine is otherwise settled.

For all motor repairs a paraffin pail is almost essential to wash all the parts in to remove grease and dirt.   A small galvanised pail, costing about 1s., and a gallon of paraffin, using half at a time, will be of the greatest use, also affording a wonderful method of cleaning the hands when the job is done.

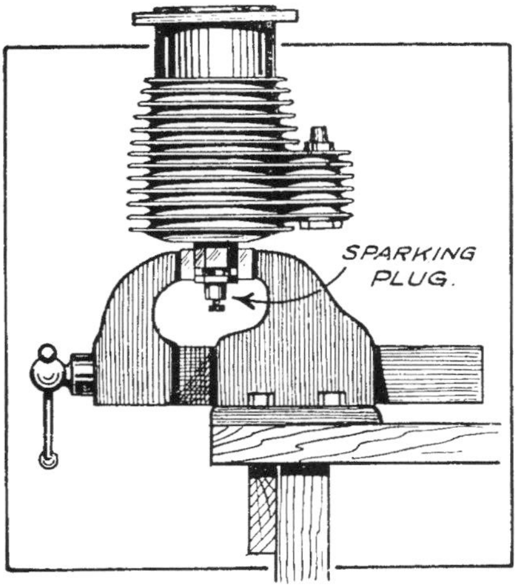

Decarbonising the Cylinder Head

When the valves are out, drop them, with the washers, springs and cotters in the paraffin while the decarbonising is got on with. For this type of cylinder it is best to purchase a set of scrapers (Fig. 15), costing 4s. 6d., as the inside of the head is awkward to get at

Fig. 16.—Cylinder held for Decarbonising by an old Sparking Plug held in Vice.

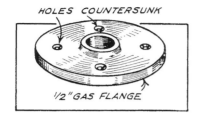

Fig. 17.—A Simple Device for Holding Cylinder.

otherwise, and it is most essential that all carbon is removed from the top of the combustion chamber, as this is the part receiving the maximum heat. Carefully clean all round the valve pockets, and the ports below the valves. If the inlet valve has been leaking, quite a lot of carbon is often found below it, but generally the exhaust valve port alone becomes dirty. Do not scratch the metal of the ports and passages more than can be helped, as this will form a key for carbon.

A Use for Old Sparking Plugs

If the special scrapers are not available, the head can be cleaned with a long screwdriver used as a scraper, the cylinder being held in the vice as shown in Fig. 16, an old sparking plug being screwed into the cylinder to hold it by if the plug hole is in the centre of the head. If not, screw in one of the valve caps, and grip this in the vice, or alternatively an old sparking plug screwed in place in the valve cap may be used.

Fig. 17A.—Sparking Plug Adapter.

Screwed ½ inch gas outside, sparking plug thread inside.

If a Vice is not Available

In many cases a vice will not be available, but it is very useful to be able to securely hold a cylinder mouth up for fitting piston rings, etc., so the simple device shown in Fig. 17 can be used on any bench or table. From an ironmongers purchase a ½-inch gas flange. Drill four ¼-inch holes and countersink these for wood screws. Use 1¼-inch No. 10 wood screws, and screw this in some convenient position on a bench or table. Then procure a sparking-plug adapter (Fig. 17A). This will be screwed ½-inch gas outside and standard sparking-plug thread inside. Screw this into the flange. Then cut off the threaded portion from an old discarded long-reach plug, and screw this on the adapter. Then the cylinder can be screwed on to this (Fig. 18), and will be quite firm for any work to be carried out. If necessary, a longer threaded portion can be used instead of the sparking-plug end. A piece of steel rod of the right diameter

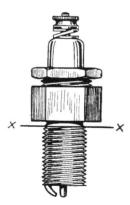

Fig. 17B.—Old Long-reach Plug

Cut off screwed part at X—X with a hacksaw.

can be screwed ½-inch gas at one end and sparking-plug thread at the other (Fig. 19).

The cylinder can then be attached by either the central sparking-plug hole or the hole in the valve plug, whichever is available. When the carbon is all removed, examine the valve seatings. If the exhaust valve has been allowed to get into bad condition, the seating in the cylinder may be burned. The method of dealing with a case like this will be given later.

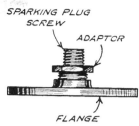

Fig. 17c.—The Complete Fitting.

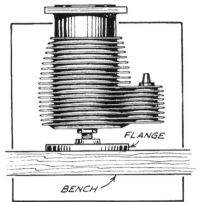

Fig. 18.—Cylinder held Mouth up for Decarbonising on Device shown in Fig. 17.

Decarbonising the Valves

Take the valves out of the paraffin, wipe them dry, and then see that the stems are quite free from scale or carbon. Carbon will sometimes be found in a thick deposit under the head of the valve (Fig. 20). Scrape off all deposit and scale, but do not scratch the stems. Then with fine emery cloth polish the stems *lengthways*, do not polish the stems as shown in Fig. 21a, as this will form rings round them and tend to hold dirt and carbon. Feel the stems carefully with the fingers to see if any wear can be felt. Worn stems appear like Fig. 22, but a very little wear will affect the running, especially in the inlet valve stem.

Examine the Valve Stems and Guides

If the valve stem is worn any appreciable amount, discard it and fit a new valve, which must still, however, be ground in to its seating. If the valve stem is worn to any extent, the valve guide is almost certain to be worn. Sometimes it is the guide which is worn and not the stem. When the valve is quite clean, clean the guide. To do this make up a swab by pinching a piece of rag or waste in a wire (Fig. 23), and then having soaked this in paraffin, force it through the guides. Then try the valve in the guide. There should be no appreciable shake.

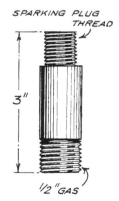

Fig. 19.—Extension Piece for Fig. 17 instead of End of old Sparking Plug.

4

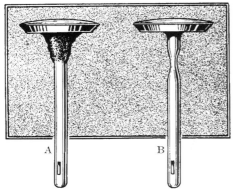

Fig. 20.—Two Valve Faults.
A, Carbon deposit under head of valve. B, burnt valve stem.

paste, sold in two grades, fine and coarse.

Grinding in the Valves

There are equally good grinding mediums, but avoid using the ordinary emery powder of commerce : it is too variable in quality and grade, and will cut rings in both valves and seatings. If the valves are little worn or pitted, place a little,

If there is considerable play the valve guide must be renewed, as leakage up the valve guide of the inlet valve will cause difficult starting and irregular running at slow speeds. If the exhaust valve guide is worn, the valve will not drop square on its seat, and will leak, causing burning of both valve and seating. It will be taken now, however, that both valves and guides are in good order, only needing grinding in. Procure a box of carborundum

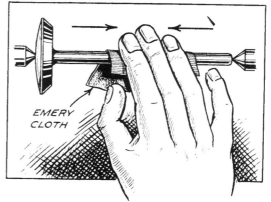

Fig. 21.—Polish Valve Stems Lengthways as Above.

just a smear, of fine carborundum paste on the seat. Drop the valve into place, and with a screwdriver or grinding tool give two or three turns to and fro. Then, keeping a finger under the stem, relax the pressure on the screwdriver, lift the valve a little by the finger under the stem, drop it, and

Fig. 21A.—Never this Way.

give two or three more turns. Repeat this until there seems, by feel, to be no "cut" in the grinding material. Then withdraw the valve, wipe the seat and seating, and examine. If there is a fine, grey, continuous

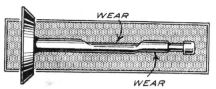

Fig. 22.—VALVE STEM WEARS.

line, not wavy, round both the valve and seating, no further grinding is necessary. Do the other valve likewise.

How to ensure a True Seating

To make quite sure that a true seat is obtained, smear a little lampblack mixed with oil—it must be a very thin smear—on the valve seat. Put in place, turn the

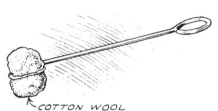

Fig. 23.—VALVE GUIDE SWAB.
Made by pulling over end of wire on to some cotton waste.

valve round once, withdraw, and see that there is a continuous line of lampblack round the seating.

Trouble is often caused by observing the valve only when grinding in. A single high place on the seating will mark the valve right round, though it will be far from making a true seat. There must be a line round both valve and seat. When seat-

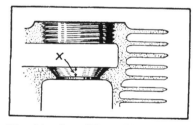

Fig. 24.—OLD WORN VALVE SEAT.
Note width of seating at X X.

ings become old and worn, the seat line becomes very wide (Fig. 24), and it is a difficult job to get and keep such a seat tight. The narrower the seat line the better, which is one reason why as little grinding as possible should be done, only enough to ensure a tight seat. The two types of valve heads are shown in A and B, Fig. 25. Any screwdriver can be used with A, but a tool like Fig. 26 must be used for B. This is sometimes provided in the tool kit, but if not, can be purchased for 2s. 6d. There is a danger with this type that the valve is turned too much

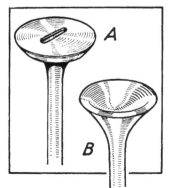

Fig. 25.—SHOWING TWO TYPES OF VALVE HEADS.
Any screwdriver can be used to grind in A, but a tool like Fig. 26 must be used for B.

Fig. 25A.—Showing Wear between Valve Stem and Guide.

without lifting it. If this is done, grooves will be cut round both seat and seating (Fig. 27), and the valve will either not hold or keep tight only for a short time. If a valve is badly worn on the seat like Fig. 28, it should be discarded. To attempt to grind this in would spoil the seating on the cylinder, a very expensive matter.

Now wash Valves and Cylinder in Paraffin

When the valves have been ground in wash them in paraffin to remove all trace of carborundum. Then wash the cylinder thoroughly both inside and outside in paraffin, with a narrow brush, cleaning thoroughly between all the fins to remove caked dust or oil which would affect the cooling efficiency.

Renew Valve Springs if they are Weak

Put the swab (Fig. 23) through the guides, and then allow the cylinder to drain before wiping. The great heat to which they are exposed often affects the valve springs, making them weak and causing irregular running and loss of power. If either spring seems weak, probably the exhaust valve spring, replace it. A new spring only costs a few pence, and a weak spring can give a lot of trouble.

Replacing the Valves

Put the springs over the guides, put the spring washer on the end of the spring and force it over the push-rod screw. Reference may be made to Fig. 13 on page 50. Next drop the valve stem through the guide, taking care that the right valve is fitted, and then apply the valve lifter and force the spring washer and spring up the stem. If the cotters are of the split-cone type (Fig. 6), put a little thick grease in the groove in the

Fig. 26.—Grinding Tool for use with Valves, Type B, Fig. 25.

stem, and this will hold the one half cotter in place while the other is fitted, and by relaxing the lifter screw the valve washer is lowered on to the cotter. In some cases, such as that in Fig. 11, the push rods and their guides are removed with the cylinder. If the push rods have been removed, replace these in the way they were taken out, as it will be noted that in a large number of cases these differ, the exhaust tappet being fitted with a large collar.

How to make a New Paper Washer

When the valves and the tappets have been replaced, the cylinder will be ready to put back on the crankcase. If the joint on the bottom flange of cylinder was broken in removing it, make another. Good smooth brown paper, the kind with a glazed finish, should be used. Hold the paper over the cylinder mouth or spigot, and with a block of wood hammer the edge all round until the paper is cut away by the sharp edge of the casting and can be pulled over the spigot.

Do not use a hammer for this, not even a copper hammer, or the edge of the cylinder spigot will be burred, and it will not enter its faucet in the crankcase. A small, light, wood mallet is the best tool for this job. Now do the same for the tappet guides if they project below the cylinder face, as in Fig. 11, and when the joint is down on the face, hammer it all round the edge with the mallet to cut it to the shape of the cylinder flange. Do not try to push the four bolt holes through the paper by forcing a bolt or some round article through it or the paper will be puckered and torn. Tap over the holes with the wood or mallet

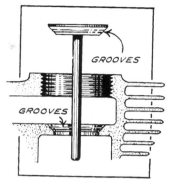

Fig. 27.—Result of Incorrect Grinding Method.

Grooves cut round valve and seat by grinding without periodically lifting the valve off its seat.

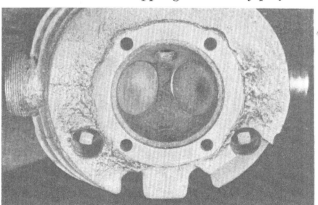

Fig. 27a.—Result of Running with Worn Inlet Valve Guide.

This cylinder head is an excellent example. Owing to the wear in the guide the valve has not been striking the seating true. The bright groove shows where the valve strikes before it actually seats, thus causing a marked loss of power, spitting back, etc.

Fig. 28.—BADLY WORN VALVE SEAT.

No attempt should be made to grind this in or the cylinder seating will be ruined. Either discard it and fit a new valve, or have it turned up in the lathe or cuttered up in a valve cutter to restore the seat.

lightly and they will be cut through by the sharp edges of the holes, or if the holes have had the edges bevelled, as in some cases to ease the cylinder on to the studs, the holes will be plainly marked, and can be cut out with a penknife while the joint is on the cylinder face.

Dealing with the Piston

The cylinder is now all ready to replace, so attention can be given to the piston. When the cylinder was removed some precautions should have been taken to support the connecting rod, as otherwise it can fall over to one side of the cylinder opening; the piston will drop as shown in Fig. 29, and if the engine is then turned, the edge of the piston will come down on to the crank chamber face, and may have its edge bent or damaged. To avoid this, when the cylinder is removed, a good and simple precaution is to twist a stout rubber band round the connecting rod and over the four studs (Fig. 30). This will maintain the connecting rod in the centre even if the engine is turned. Another plan is to cut two strips of wood as shown in Fig. 31, and slip them over the studs, the slot in the centre supporting the connecting rod. One drawback to this method is that the engine cannot be turned completely round if it is desired to do so, as the piston skirt will come on to the wood, but this is an excellent method to support the piston while it is being cleaned and having the piston rings taken off and replaced, as otherwise it flops about with every touch and makes the work difficult (see Fig. 29).

Fig. 29.—DON'T ALLOW THIS.

Skirt of piston is liable to damage if left unsupported with cylinder off and engine is turned. (See Figs. 30–34A.)

Fig. 30.—METHOD OF SUPPORTING CONNECTING ROD.

Two rubber bands used to support connecting rod when cylinder is removed.

Polish the Top if you like

Scrape the top of the piston quite clean, taking care not to scratch the metal. A tool with a sharp smooth edge is best for this, such as a wood chisel. Clean also the small " land " between the top piston ring and the head of the piston (Fig. 32). Some riders polish the head of the piston after cleaning. This can be done or not as desired : a good metal polish makes the best medium.

Rings and Grooves

If the piston and cylinder are badly carbonised, it is advisable to remove the

Fig. 32.—WHEN CLEANING TOP OF PISTON.

Also clean the top " land " XX, even if rings are not removed.

piston and clean the rings and grooves, also the inside head of the piston. There are many different methods of securing the gudgeon pin (see " Dismantling "), and when the piston is removed it must be treated very gently indeed to avoid damage. A fall on to the floor would probably mean a new piston, and it must not be held in the vice or it will be distorted and ruined.

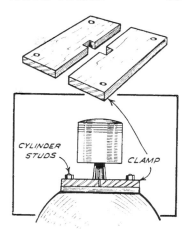

Fig. 31.—ANOTHER METHOD OF SUPPORTING CONNECTING ROD.

Wood strips to keep connecting rod in centre when cylinder is off. If desired, piston can be pulled down on to wood strips by rotating the engine. This will render piston firm for removing rings and cleaning.

A Piston Clamp—for the Garage Man

Where large numbers of pistons have to be handled, a piston clamp, as shown in Fig. 33, is used. This is adjustable to take a wide range of sizes, and quite avoids any damage to the piston. This, however, is an expensive tool, costing about 25s., and the private rider would not be justified in purchasing it, but all garages should have this tool, as its cost would be more than covered by spoiling two pistons.

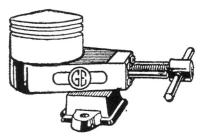

Fig. 33.—PISTON CLAMP.

Allows piston to be held without damage, and covers a large range of diameters.

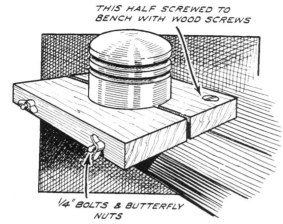

*THIS HALF SCREWED TO
BENCH WITH WOOD SCREWS*

*1/4" BOLTS & BUTTERFLY
NUTS*

Fig. 34.—A SIMPLE AND INEXPENSIVE PISTON
CLAMP.
This enables piston to be held either way up
without damage.

For the Owner Driver

For the owner rider a simple holder can be made as follows, and will be very useful. Procure a piece of wood, oak or ash is best, about 6 inches square and 1½ inches thick. Mark a circle on this with a pair of compasses or dividers the same diameter as the piston. Then mark a line across the diameter square with the sides, and continue over the edges. Mark two points on each edge equidistant from centre line and to clear the piston diameter by about ⅜ inch. Then with an auger bit or twist drill held in a breast brace bore two holes right through the wood.

It is better to start from each side, as the holes will have less chance of running out. The holes should be $\frac{5}{16}$-inch diameter. With a wood saw cut the wood in halves as shown, and then with a keyhole or pad saw cut out the two half circles. At an ironmonger's purchase two ¼-inch diameter bolts 7 inches long, and two ¼-inch butterfly nuts and two washers, about 8*d*. the lot. The bolts should be of the type known as "round-square-square," and the square nuts are discarded. Screw one

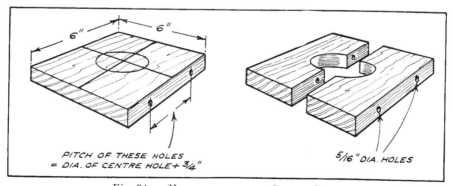

6"   *6"*

*PITCH OF THESE HOLES
= DIA. OF CENTRE HOLE + 3/4"*

5/16" DIA. HOLES

Fig. 34A.—HOW TO MAKE THE PISTON CLAMP.
Giving the dimensions and method of marking out. Fig. 34 shows the clamp in use.

of the halves to the bench as shown, put the bolts through both halves, and the piston can be clipped without chance of damage, either way up (Fig. 34).

If a wood turner is available, have the hole in the wood bored out in the lathe, it will make a cleaner job. As the total cost of the clip should not exceed 1s., several could be made in the case of pistons of different diameters being handled.

Removing the Rings

To remove the rings, take several pieces of sheet tin about $1\frac{1}{2}$ inches long and $\frac{3}{8}$ inch wide. With a sharp-pointed tool lift one of the ends of the top ring out of the slot and put a strip of tin under it. Slip this round until opposite the slot in the ring. Then put another strip of tin under

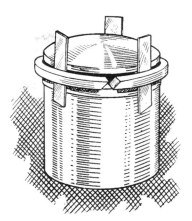

Fig. 35.—METHOD OF REMOVING RINGS.

Slip strips of tin under the rings. Work them round from the split until spaced equally apart. The ring can then be slid up the strips off the piston. Handle carefully. Piston rings are very delicate things.

each end of the ring, which will now appear like Fig. 35. It can then be slipped off the piston.

Do the next ring likewise ; the strips of tin will form bridges to prevent this ring falling into the top ring groove. If available, an old hacksaw blade broken into short pieces will do instead of the strips of tin. Scrape the rings clean inside where the carbon has lodged, and see that the edges are clean.

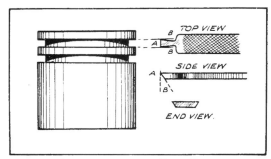

Fig. 36.—TO CLEAN RING SLOTS.
Grind the end of a small flat file like as at AA. Draw this end of the file round the grooves. Note clearances to form cutting edges. The end A must be a good fit to the grooves in width.

Cleaning

Next clean out the grooves in the piston. If a wood chisel narrow enough to enter the grooves is available, the grooves can be cleaned out with this. Otherwise grind the end of a small file like Fig. 36, and draw this through the grooves. In the case of air-cooled two-stroke engines using petroil, the top ring may

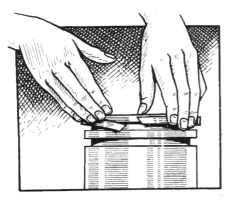

Fig. 37.—Method of replacing Rings by Hand.

Hold one end firmly on piston, and move the other end down across the top slot. Then hold the latter end tightly while moving the other down. Repeat until ring is over its slot, then let it drop in.

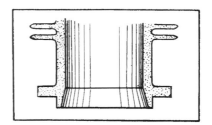

Fig. 38.—For easy fitting of Piston into Cylinder.

Mouth of cylinder bevelled to allow it to slip over piston rings.

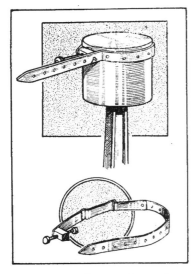

Fig. 39.—A Piston Ring Compressor.

Adjustable band for compressing piston rings when replacing the cylinder. The cylinder pushes the band off as it is lowered down.

become so firmly carbonised in its groove that it can only be broken out and a new ring fitted. Directions on fitting new rings will be given later.

How to replace the Rings

After the rings and slots are clean, replace the rings, taking care not to break them. Start with the bottom ring first. Slip this over the top of the piston, holding the two ends firmly to prevent them falling into the top slot. Move one end down across the top slot. Hold this and move the other end down below this. Do this alternately until the ring drops into its own slot (Fig. 37). When the rings are in place, turn the piston over in the clip, and then with a sharp-ended tool, such as a screwdriver, clean off all the carbon from the inside of the crown and round the sides. If the set of cleaning tools shown in Fig. 15 are available, these can, of course, be used.

Reassembly

When the piston is quite clean, give it a wash in the paraffin pail to remove any trace of grit, etc. See that the rings are free in the slots, as after having removed and replaced them they sometimes tend to bind. Replace the piston on the connecting rod, oiling the gudgeon pin well before inserting.

Replacing the Cylinder

Now prepare to replace the cylinder. Coat the paper washer or gasket with goldsize, or one of the proprietary jointing materials, on both sides, taking care not to tear it, and press it evenly down over the cylinder studs. It is better to coat the gasket than the two faces, as there is then less chance of surplus jointing getting into the crankcase, etc. The mouth of the cylinder is usually bevelled to enable it to pass over the rings (Fig. 38), and with a little manipulation this can usually be accomplished without any ring compressor being used. First see that the joints in the rings do not come opposite ; separate them as far as possible round the piston. Then if the top ring is pinched in with the fingers of one hand, the cylinder can be lowered over it with the other, each ring being treated in this way. Well oil both the piston and the bore of cylinder before replacing.

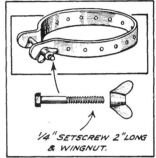

Fig. 40.—A Cheap Piston-ring Clip.

Made from a Meccano strip.

For Difficult Cases

In some cases the bevel is not enough to allow the rings to enter without being fully compressed, and then a tool of the kind shown in Fig. 39 must be used. The action will be clear from the sketch. It is clipped lightly round the piston, tight enough to quite compress the ring but not enough to grip on the piston. The cylinder, in its descent, pushes the clip off, but not until the ring has passed into the bore. Clips can be made up for a few pence, using a strip of Meccano steel, as in Fig. 40, and a screw and nut. When the cylinder is over the piston guide it carefully on to the studs, and see that it settles evenly on the paper gasket. Then put on the nuts and tighten evenly, giving each nut a part turn in order, finally pulling each down deadtight.

Fig. 41.—Feeler Gauge.

With various clearances given on blades. Usually supplied in tool kits.

Adjusting the Valves

It is now necessary to adjust the lift or clearance of the valves. A feeler gauge is often included in the tool kit with blades of the correct thickness, but if not, one must be purchased (Fig. 41). These can be got at all prices: one multiple store even sells one at 6*d*.

How to test Tappet Clearances

On side-by-side valve engines the inlet valve clearance is generally about ·002 inch, and the exhaust ·004 inch, but whatever clearance the

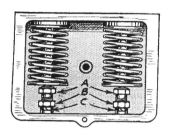

Fig. 42.—VALVE TAPPET SCREWS.

To loosen tappet screws A, the tappets must be held by the flats on them C, and also when the lock nuts B are tightened.

makers give should be adhered to. Turn the engine, and note when the inlet valve tappet is right down—at the bottom of its stroke. Test the clearance with the correct blade of the feeler gauge. If it needs correction, and it will after the valves have been reground, hold the head of the tappet screw A, Fig. 42, with one of the spanners provided, and loosen the lock nut B. Then screw the tappet screw in or out as required, holding the tappet C by another spanner the while. Test the clearance, and when correct, tighten the lock nut B. Test again, and it will probably be found that the clearance has altered: the tightening of the lock nut is apt to affect it.

Repeat until the correct clearance is obtained. Turn the engine round several times, and again try the clearance. When in order see that

the lock nut B is as tight as it can be got. Then set the other tappet in the same way. If it is the exhaust tappet make sure that the lifter is quite free, as if this is affecting the tappet the correct clearance will not be obtained. Look to the valve cover joint, renewing it if in bad condition, and replace the valve cover and tighten up. After the first run again check the tappet clearance, as the valves tend to get bedded in and a small clearance like ·002 inch may be wiped out by this and the valve held open all the time.

TWO-STROKE ENGINES

As previously stated, two-stroke engines need more frequent decarbonising than four-stroke. There are

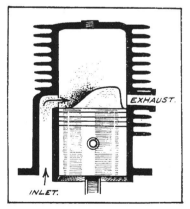

Fig. 43.—A POINT TO WATCH FOR CARBON DEPOSIT.

Section of two-stroke cylinder, showing oil spray impinging on piston deflector with incoming charge.

two reasons for this. Double the number of explosions take place in a two-stroke than in a four-stroke cylinder for any given number of revolutions.

Why Two-stroke needs more Frequent Decarbonising

The lubrication of such engines is usually by oil mixed with the petrol, so that a good deal more lubricating oil is burned above the piston than in a

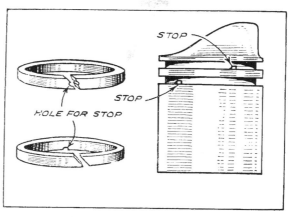

Fig. 44.—Look for Ring Stops.

Two-stroke piston, showing stops in piston ring grooves to prevent them turning and the slots getting into line.

four-stroke engine. The exhaust gases, too, are less completely expelled, and if the charge is first taken into the crankcase, as in most models, there is a considerable amount of oil impinged directly on to the deflector on the piston crown (Fig. 43), where it is burned to carbon. If left too long, the piston rings, especially the top one, may have to be broken to get it out.

When the rings are removed, clean the grooves well, and especially the top of piston and deflector. The inside of the cylinder head will also need cleaning, and the exhaust port and passage (Fig. 43) must receive a thorough cleaning. The transfer port seldom needs attention.

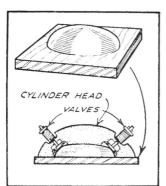

Fig. 45.—While Springs are being Compressed.

Block of wood shaped to fit inside cylinder head and hold valves.

On two-stroke engines it is essential that the joints in the rings should not come opposite, as if they should do so, some of the hot gases in the firing stroke might pass into the inlet port and cause firing in the crank chamber. To avoid this, the rings are generally fitted with slots (Fig. 44).

Care with the Cylinder Joint

The type shown in Fig. 44, with the slot at the joint of the ring, is best, as the slot for the stop on the edge of the ring (see also Fig. 44) is liable to cause the ring to break at that point, especially when removing or replacing it. With these pistons a clip will be advisable for the rings (Figs. 39 and 40), as if the cylinder is replaced without one, the ends of the rings tend to get over the small stops and make the ring project beyond the piston, so that it is liable to be broken when putting the cylinder on. The cylinder flange joint must be very carefully made with a two-stroke engine, as leakage from the crank

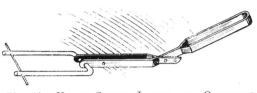

Fig. 46.—VALVE SPRING LIFTER FOR OVERHEAD VALVES.

chamber will affect the power seriously. Some do not use any jointing material on the cylinder gasket for four-stroke engines, but this must not be omitted on two-stroke. Two-stroke air-cooled engines should be decarbonised frequently : they will not run as long as four-stroke, and serious damage will be done to the piston and cylinder if it is neglected too long.

OVERHEAD VALVE ENGINES

The task of decarbonising overhead valve engines, with detachable heads, and regrinding the valves, is much easier than with solid-head cylinders. Having removed the head, lay it on a bench or table.

Make up a block of wood which will just fit evenly in the combustion chamber, like Fig. 45. This can be roughly shaped with a rasp, and need not fit the combustion chamber exactly. Its purpose is to hold the heads of the valves when the spring is compressed (Fig. 45), which makes it much easier to remove the springs and cotters.

Compressing the Valve Springs

For compressing the springs a different type of valve

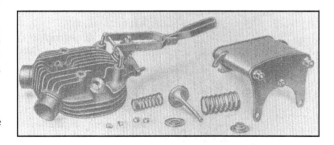

Fig. 46A.—VALVE LIFTER IN ACTION.
One valve is shown removed (Ariel).

lifter must be used than for side-by-side valves. One of these is illustrated in Fig. 46, and Fig. 46A shows the lifter in action. There are several types of lifters for overhead valves ; in some engines, owing to special points in the design, only one form of lifter can be used, and this is generally supplied in the tool kit by the makers.   Compress the springs by the lifter, remove the cotters, and then having removed the lifter, take off the spring and spring washer and then push the valve stem through the guide and remove the valve (Fig. 46A). When the valves are all out, turn the head over and remove all the carbon with a scraper (Fig. 47A). Clean all the valve ports and passages, taking care not to scratch the metal.   The head is a very delicate part, and should be handled carefully or ribs may be broken off.

Fig. 47.—Inside View of a Four-valve Head.

Showing valve seats and ports.

To hold it securely for decarbonising, the device shown in Fig. 16 can be used.   The regrinding operation does not differ from that of side-by-side valves, but is more conveniently carried out, as the job can be done on the bench.   When the work on the head is finished, the piston can be decarbonised, and in this case there is no need to remove the cylinder unless other work is required. The piston is brought to the top of the cylinder and the carbon can then be cleaned off.   Before replacing the head, see that the joint faces of both the head and the cylinder are clean.

Replacing the Head

On some engines no joint washer is used here, so clean off any old jointing compound that may be adhering.   Scrape it off, leaving the

Fig. 47A.—Polishing the Cylinder Head and Valve Ports by means of a Specially Bent File.   (*Raleigh.*)

faces clean and smooth. Then coat one of the faces with goldsize or any of the usual jointing compounds, and put the head in place. Then tighten down the bolts slightly, tightening those diagonally opposite, and going round in this order, 1, 3, 2, 4, giving each a part turn until all are tight, thus ensuring that the head is pulled down quite evenly. On some engines a copper ring gasket is fitted in a groove in the head. If this is in good order it can be used several times. Take it carefully out of the groove, lay it on a flat surface, and scrape off any old jointing compound. Also clean out the groove in the head and the spigot on the cylinder. Then coat the washer with jointing compound and replace.

Engines with side-by-side valves and detachable heads (Fig. 48) are the most convenient to work on. There are no special points about either valve grinding or decarbonising. The head joint is made with a copper asbestos gasket as in most motor-car engines. This will serve many times if care is taken when breaking the joint. Clean and treat as in the last case. When tightening down the head, start at bolt or stud No. 1, and work round clockwise, tightening each bolt the same amount, say one sixth turn, until all are of equal tightness.

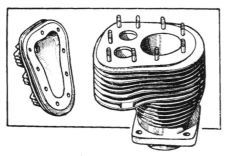

Fig. 48.—Easy to work on.

Engines with detachable heads of this type have a copper asbestos gasket for making the joint which must be handled very carefully or it will be spoiled.

Test the Compression

With all types, when the work is completed, turn the engine round and test the compression. If poor, one of the valves is probably held up by a piece of dirt or carbon. Turn the valves round in their seats while they are open, then again test the compression. Loss of compression can be caused, after this work has been carried out on the engine, by (1) leaky valves either not properly ground in or dirt having got under them ; (2) leaky head joint ; (3) leaky rings. The latter can be disregarded for the present, and the remedy for the two first is obvious.

Valve Setting of Overhead Valves.

This does not differ in method from that of side-by-side valves, but the clearance is generally less. On some engines no clearance at all is allowed. In these cases, test the compression after taking up all the clearance. If the compression is satisfactory the valves are seating, but if not, one of the valves is probably set up too tight, and must be slightly released. The best plan is to test the compression first with the valves having clearance, which will prove if the valves and head joint are tight. Then set up the valves until there is no clearance and again test.

What to do with the De-compressor Valve on Two-stroke Engines

On most two-stroke engines, having no exhaust valve to lift to ease the compression, there is a de-compressor fitted, a small valve in a detachable seat, which will be seen in Fig. 49, screwed into the head. Leakage of compression after decarbonising may be due to leakage of this valve, which should be removed and ground in each time the engine is decarbonised. The port in connection with this valve should also be cleaned, the best method being to pass a twist drill the same dia-meter as the port through it. Graphite the thread of the valve housing when replacing, or it will be hard to detach next time.

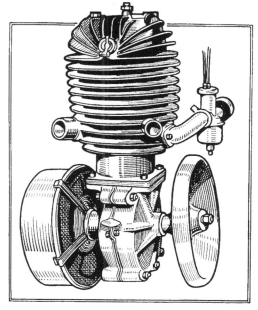

Fig. 49.—Two-stroke with Decompressor Valve.

This valve in the front of the head, and its ports need cleaning and the valve grinding in at intervals.

How to treat Threads for Easy Unscrewing

The threads of all valve plugs, head bolts, nuts, etc., or any threads exposed to great heat should be well coated with graphite mixed with oil, so that they can be easily unscrewed at any time. Do not use some of the graphite jointing pastes sold, as these are intended to make permanent joints, such as on gas and steam pipes, and do not have the same effect as graphite and oil only.

5

REPAIR AND MAINTENANCE OF RUDGE ENGINES

By B. P. RANSOM (*Rudge Whitworth, Ltd.*)

Fig. 1.—ADJUSTING TAPPETS (1931 ULSTER).
Note the tappet-rod cover is lifted clear after the nut, which secures this by the slotted lug, has been slackened off.

OVERHAUL AND ADJUSTMENT OF POWER UNIT

Inspect your Tappets Regularly

COMMENCING with the engine, very regular inspection of tappet adjustments is desirable. These should be adjusted when the engine is cold, and should be so set that the push rod rotates freely between the fingers, but has no perceptible up-and-down movement. If a tight spot is felt when the rod is rotated, it means that either tappet or push rod is bent, and if it is not found practicable to straighten them they should be replaced.

The inlet should be run thus—the exhaust should be adjusted back to give ·002 inch clearance (Fig. 1). If the clearance is allowed to become excessive, hammering results, and wear on the overhead rockers may be expected.

Fig. 2.—Tightening Cylinder Head Bolts.
Give each bolt half a turn at a time.   Note the front right-hand bolt partly screwed up.

Types of Rockers

The 1928 and 1929 special overhead rockers were of the barrel type, with internal rollers. If it is found necessary to remove these from the head, when replacing them the rollers should be secured in place with thick grease, and the spindle introduced before fitting to the head.

The 1930 and 1931 heads have rocker-bearing supports cast integral with them, and the previous arrangement of rollers is reversed, as in this case they run on the rockers and in races pressed into the supports. A small amount of endplay in the overhead rockers is unimportant, but undue lift makes tappet adjustment difficult, and should be eliminated by the replacement of rollers, which will usually be sufficient to correct matters.

Fig. 3.—DETACHING HEAD, FIRST STAGE.

Note the rocker-box cover is removed. The exhaust lifter adjuster, which also secures the tappet-rod cover, is disconnected. The cylinder head bolts are unscrewed so that the head may be raised (1930 Rudge Special).

Points to Note on Cylinder Head Joints

The joint between the cylinder head and barrel is made with a copper asbestos washer, prior to 1930, when the plain copper gasket was introduced. Great care is needed in tightening the head bolts (Fig. 2). If one is pulled up first, it will be hopeless to expect to make a gastight joint. It is better to go round the head, giving each bolt half a turn at a time. The tapped holes in the head are blind, therefore it is as well to make sure the bolts are the correct length, as if one bottoms, it is quite possible to twist it off. Do not forget that these bolts are too long to enter their respective holes after the cylinder has been bolted to the crankcase, and consequently should be put in place before the cylinder is replaced.

The Cylinder Head

The cylinder head should be carefully examined. It is important to note the positions of the four valves, and to replace each one in its original seating. If the engine has run any length of time, it is possible that the valve guides, or at any rate the inlet guides, will need replacing. In this case, the seatings should be recut—and in any case if a cutter is available, this will reduce the labour of grinding in to a minimum.

Cutting Valve Seatings

One should take great care not to remove more metal than is necessary to just clean up the seat, for if the cutter goes too deep the opening of the valve will be masked, with consequent loss of performance. If, when the valves are ground in and refitted, it is found that one rocker arm touches a little before the other, this should be rectified by filing a little from the end of the longer valve stem.

This does not apply to the radial valve 350-c.c. and 250-c.c. models of 1931, in which case the matter can be rectified by independent adjustment of the rocker pillars.

Polished Ports

The Ulster and all racing engines are turned out with the interior of the cylinder head polished, and the ports streamlined. The firm are prepared to carry out this work on other models for a reasonable charge.

The condition of the valve springs should be noted. The correct poundage for Ulster and racing 500-c.c. engines is 80,

Fig. 4.—Removing Head of 1930 Special.

while the most suitable spring for the special is 60 lb. at half of lift of valve.

Special Clearances are Allowed

It will be noted, on removing the cylinder barrel, that the piston clearance is considerable. This is quite in order. The Rudge engine has been developed from racing experience, and it has been found advisable to allow quite a perceptible amount of play at vital points.

Another of these points is the big-end bearing. This " slop " is one of the factors which allow the Rudge engine to be driven so hard and for such long periods without showing symptoms of tiredness.

Reducing Endplay on Early Models

The 1928 engines and all 1929 engines except the Ulster had a two-bearing crankshaft. These bearings were merely pressed into the crankcase. After long usage occasionally it is found that a little endplay develops on the crankshaft. This is taken up by fitting extra washers between the flywheels and the bearings. The first washer should be put on the driving side, the second on the timing, and so on. A range of suitable washers of various thicknesses can be obtained from the firm.

Fig. 5.—ADJUSTING EXHAUST LIFTER ON 1931 ULSTER MODEL.

Notes on Fly-wheels

It is not possible for the amateur to dismantle and satisfactorily re-erect his flywheels, and if attention to the big end is necessary the whole flywheel assembly should be returned to the works. The four tapers are there pulled up by special tackle very considerably more securely than is possible outside.

The 1929 Ulster engine and all subsequent models have a three-bearing crankshaft. There is one ball and one roller bearing on the drive side, and a roller bearing on the timing side. The ball bearing is outside and is pressed into the crankshaft first. This is locked into place with a screwed ring, the removal of which may present difficulties, unless a length of hexagon steel 5 or 6 inches long and $1\frac{5}{16}$ inches across the flats be available. One end can be introduced into the hexagon hole in the locking ring, and the other gripped by a large adjustable spanner, when the ring can be unscrewed without difficulty. There is a short tubular distance piece between the two bearings on the left-hand side. It is

Fig. 6.—Setting the Decompressor Lever of 1931 Ulster.
This fitting affords easing starting. The lever is fitted to a serrated shaft.

Fig. 7.—CYLINDER BARREL REMOVED, SHOWING THE COMPRESSION PLATE.

most important that this be replaced—the consequences of omission are disastrous.   The small timing pinion is secured to the right-hand axle by a taper and right-hand nut.   It is not advisable to attempt to remove this pinion unless an extractor is available.

The shock absorber on the left-hand axle requires but little attention. It is lubricated by an oilway drilled up the axle.   The end nut should, however, be locked up very securely indeed.

Compression Ratios—a Warning *re* Compression Plates

The majority of Rudge engines are provided with one or more compression plates under the cylinder base (Fig. 7).   In some cases these may be removed for tuning purposes, and in others this is not possible.

The 1929 Ulster engine is a case in point.   This engine has a compression ratio of 6·5 with the plate in position, and the clearance between piston and valves is so small that if the plate be removed there is grave danger of them fouling each other, with consequent risk of a wrecked piston and bent valves.   This danger would of course be accentuated by the inadvertent use of the exhaust valve lifter while the engine was revving, or the possibility of a sticking valve.

A Useful Tip for checking Clearance between Piston and Valves

In any case, when removing a plate, it is advisable to check the clearances carefully.   This may be done by sticking a piece of plasticine to the piston top and slowly rotating the engine by hand.   The thickness of plasticine at the greatest depth of the indentation made by the valves of course then represents the clearance. It may also be necessary to obtain shorter push rods if more than one plate is to be removed.

How to measure the Compression Ratio of an Engine

A compression ratio of 7·25 should not be exceeded for use with petrol-benzole mixture, while 8·25 is about the maximum possible. This can of course only be employed with alcohol fuels. The compression ratio is most conveniently measured by pouring oil from a graduated measuring glass into the central plug hole while the piston is at the top of the stroke. Allow time for the oil on the inside of the glass to drain back, and note the amount required to fill the cylinder head. With a 500-c.c. engine, 80 c.c. would represent a ratio of approximately 7·25, while 69 c.c. would be about 8·25. A compression plate ·1 inch in thickness represents 14 c.c. with an 85-mm. bore. Do not forget that to obtain the full advantage of an increased compression ratio, it will be necessary to readjust the carburetter and to increase the jet sizes.

Ignition Timing

The most suitable ignition timing for all touring 500-c.c. engines is for the points to break between 35° and 39° before top dead centre when the control is fully advanced. In the case of Ulster and racing engines, this may be increased to 45°. The 350-c.c. engines should be timed to break from 39° to 42° before top.

Valve Timing Details

The tappets should be set to a clearance of ·020 inch, and the exhaust valve should then open 54° before bottom dead centre, and close 17° after top. The inlet should open 2° before top, and close 41° after bottom. The timing having been set as nearly as above as is practicable, the tappets should then be readjusted, allowing no perceptible clearance on the inlet, and ·002 inch clearance on the exhaust.

All 350-c.c. touring engines from 1929 to 1931 are timed as follows :

Set the tappets to a clearance of ·015 inch, and time the exhaust valve to open 70° before bottom, and to close on top dead centre. The inlet should then open 22° before top, and close 24° after bottom.

The Ulster engines from 1929 to 1931, all dirt-track engines, and the 1931 T.T. Replica are timed thus :

The tappets are set to a clearance of ·010 inch and the exhaust should open 56° before bottom, and close 36° after top. The inlet should open 36° before top and close 56° after bottom.

In all cases it will be found more convenient to time from the bottom of the stroke—that is to say, if the exhaust opening is correct the others will follow.

The Rudge gearbox and clutch, cycle parts and lubrication system, are dealt with fully under appropriate headings later.

GENERAL NOTES ON DISMANTLING

By J. Earney, M.I.M.T.

Fig. 1.—A Very Effective Method of dealing with a Sprocket Nut.
It will be noted that the sprockets are prevented from turning by a spanner being interposed between the teeth, against the direction of rotation, whichever way it may be. A well-fitting box spanner with a long tommy bar is used to unscrew the nut. The engine is 3·48 Sturmey-Archer, fitted to a Dunelt machine.

IT is proposed to deal with this subject from a general point of view as applying to most types of machines, leaving special instructions concerning individual makes under separate headings.

Preparation

The need for cleanliness cannot be overstressed, therefore before stripping the machine should be thoroughly cleaned and all road grit and dirt removed. Paraffin is invaluable for this operation, although a number prefer petrol or benzole, particularly for the engine and the gearbox. Have several good strong boxes handy into which can be placed the parts as they are stripped from the machine. A good supply of clean rag, preferably of the " non-fluffy " variety, should also be available.

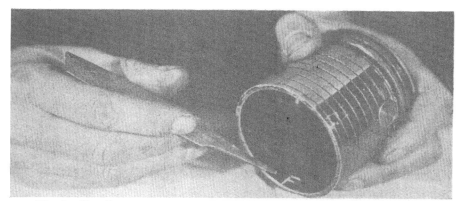

Fig. 2.—The Piston should always be replaced the Same Way Round as Originally Fitted.

The piston is marked " F," indicating this side should be fitted forwards.

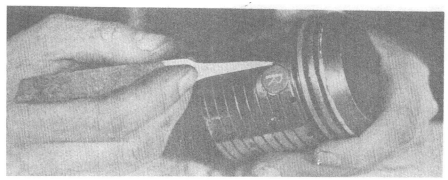

Fig. 3.—Gudgeon-pin Marking.

The gudgeon pin is marked to ensure this being refitted the same way as taken out.

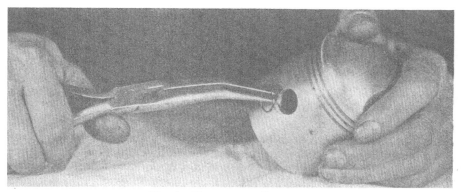

Fig. 4.—Removing a Circlip.

Illustrates a piston (Levis o.h.v. model) which has the gudgeon pin secured by circlips. The circlip has just been withdrawn, and the groove into which this is fitted will be noted.

79

ENGINE

Cylinder

The engine should be started and gradually warmed up. This will not only help to loosen nuts and unions, but also thin out the oil in the crankcase, which may be drained into some receptacle.

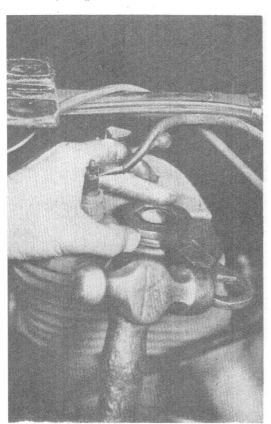

Fig. 5.—Removing Valve Caps of a S.V. Engine.

A good-fitting ring spanner, aided with a sharp blow from a hammer, is used. The machine is 3·49 B.S.A.

A Note on Valve Caps

Should it be anticipated that the valve caps are likely to be very obstinate, these may be treated overnight. A mixture of paraffin, to which a little engine oil has been added, or preferably one of the special preparations of penetrating oil, should be liberally applied to the threads.

Unions

Soaked rags may also be wound round the valve caps and exhaust pipe unions should these be of the screwed type. The heat from the warm cylinder will assist the paraffin to loosen the threads. Proceed to disconnect oil and petrol pipes, carburetter and exhaust system.

Exhaust Pipes

Where exhaust pipes are held to the cylinder by a screwed union nut trouble is very often met in unscrewing this. If the nut does not respond to reasonable persuasion, file through the nut and split this off rather than risk breaking off the exhaust port of the cylinder. The nut at the most will mean 2s., whilst a cylinder may cost £5.

Engine Sprockets

It is a good tip to unscrew the engine sprocket nut before disconnecting the chain. Should this be at all stiff, a spanner or similar tool

Fig. 6.—THE " PINCH-BOLT " METHOD OF SECURING THE GUDGEON PIN.

The bolt clamping the split ends of the connecting-rod " small end " together is shown with the " eared " lock washer. The white rod in the foreground is a cylinder bolt. The machine is a P. & M. Panther.

can be jammed between the sprocket teeth of the engine and clutch sprocket, thus allowing full power to be exerted on the nut with a box spanner and a long tommy bar, at the same time preventing the engine shaft rotating (see Fig. 1).

Rocker Gear

Some mechanics at this stage prefer to remove the remainder of engine bodily from the frame, particularly in the case of an o.h.v. model, where the rocker gear is close under the tank. The advantages are rather doubtful, as with the engine bolted in the frame considerably more leverage can be used on refractory nuts and bolts than on the bench. In any case, where the rocker gear is close to the tank the latter can quite easily be removed first.

Valve Caps, Compression Tap

With a side valve model the valve caps, compression tap, etc., can be removed. This may be easier said than done, but they will usually respond to the foregoing treatment, assisted with a good-fitting ring spanner and a few well-directed blows from a hammer (see Fig. 5). There have been extreme cases of where the corners of the hexagons have previously been worn off through ill-fitting tools, when it has been necessary to drill out the caps piecemeal after the cylinder has been removed.

Removing the Cylinder

The cylinder may now be removed. Lift this up just sufficiently to allow a clean rag to be wrapped over the crankcase orifice, thus preventing any broken rings dropping into the base when the cylinder is lifted right off—a very annoying trouble when it is not proposed to strip the crankcase. Lift the cylinder up and backwards towards the rear of the machine, then turn the engine forwards and so withdraw the piston, steadying this, to avoid damage against the connecting rod.

A Note on Twin-cylinder Engines

Some twin-cylinder designs do not allow the cylinder to be removed clear of the piston. Then the cylinder should be lifted until the gudgeon

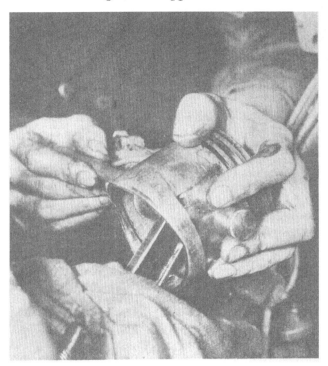

Fig. 7.—REMOVING A FLOATING GUDGEON PIN.

This photograph shows how it is usually possible to remove the gudgeon pin of the "full floating" type fitted to an aluminium piston, by pushing this out with just hand pressure. This is a 4·93 B.S.A.

pin is exposed. Drive out the pin and slip the piston farther into the cylinder until the skirt is level with the cylinder base ; this can then be easily lifted clear.

Dealing with Overhead Valve Engines

In o.h.v. models designs vary somewhat, but generally where the rocker assembly can be removed as a unit it is better to do so. Should the exhaust lifter operate direct on the cylinder head this should be discon-

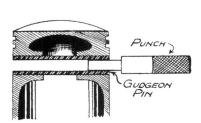

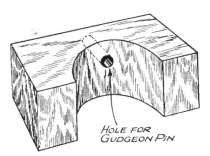

Fig. 8.—Sketch of Punch for Removing Gudgeon Pins.

Fig. 9.—Wooden Block, Recommended for supporting Piston when driving out Gudgeon Pin with a Punch, Drilled to take Pin when driven out.

nected first. The easiest way to do this is by rotating the engine until the exhaust valve is open ; this will give a fair amount of slackness to the cable, allowing the nipple to be disconnected from the lever on the cylinder head. Then by unscrewing the adjuster the control cable complete can be removed. Unscrew the holding-down bolts or nuts, and lift off the cylinder head. Should it be necessary to prise this off, take care not to damage the cylinder fins or joint face.

Always mark the Tappet Rods

It is advisable to mark the tappet push rods so that these are assembled in the same order. One small nick on the inlet and two on the exhaust with a fine file. Some makers mark them " Right " and " Left." In other cases the rods if transposed will not allow the exhaust lifter to operate, although the engine will still function. It is as well perhaps at this stage to stress the need for marking all parts where there is the slightest doubt of interchangeability. A little intelligence used in this direction when dismantling may avoid endless trouble when re-erecting the units. The methods used in securing the various parts, ear washers and locking plates, etc., should be carefully noted.

Removing Pistons and Gudgeon Pins

Before removing the piston, this should be marked. A letter " F " indicating " front " should be scratched with a scriber, just inside the piston skirts, facing forward. There are many types of gudgeon pin fixing.

Types of Gudgeon Pin Fixings

The most popular is propably the floating type, which is usually fitted with aluminium, brass, or copper end pads. These are parallel, and may be pushed out from either side. It is advisable to mark the end pad on the right-hand side with a letter " R " before removal.

In other cases the gudgeon pin is retained in position by a wire circlip, which is fitted to either side. These are located in grooves just inside the piston bosses ; after these have been removed the pin can be pushed out from either side.

Another type is that as fitted to the 250 c.c. Ariel. The end of the connecting rod is split and a set bolt clamps the gudgeon pin. The former is secured by an eared lock washer. To remove the pin it is necessary to undo the lock washer, slacken the bolt and push out the pin.

In the earlier type of cast-iron piston the gudgeon pin is usually tapered and driven into the piston. The piston is marked " in " and " out," either just over the piston bosses or on the crown. In this case the pin is driven out from the side marked " out." The use of a gudgeon pin extractor is strongly recommended (see Figs. 8 and 14). Otherwise it will be necessary to use a hammer and punch. If this method is resorted to it is most essential that the piston should be well supported by an assistant with a wooden block cut to shape as near as possible to conform to the circumference of the piston, drilled to accommodate the pin as this is

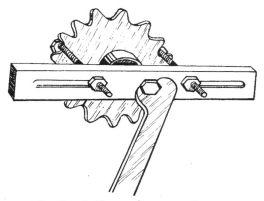

Fig. 10.—A Handy Sprocket Drawer.

driven out (see Fig. 9). Care should be taken to avoid distorting the piston or straining the connecting rod. Another type of fixing employed with cast-iron pistons is by split pin, dowel or grub screw, which is in turn secured by a wire. There is also a type retained by a flat band like a very wide piston ring.

The method employed by the B.S.A. Co. with the cast-iron pistons is by a patent spring ring fitted to the pin, which locates in a groove in the piston. The pin is removed by hammer and punch as previously directed, driving out from that end of the pin with the larger hole. The punch used to drive out gudgeon pins should be slightly smaller than the pin, and should have the end turned down to enter the pin (see Fig. 8).

How to remove the Engine Sprocket

The nut holding the sprocket to the engine shaft has already been taken off and the sprocket may now be removed. Where a cush drive is fitted this assembly should be detached intact, thus allowing the

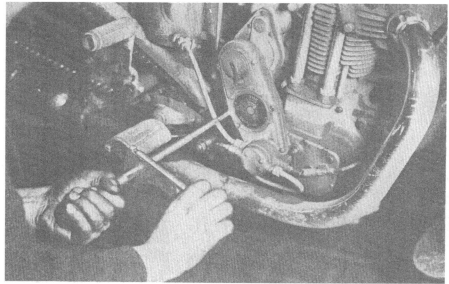

Fig. 11.—Removing the Timing Case Screws.

The screws are being removed, and the method of exerting additional leverage with a wrench on the shank of a long screwdriver is shown. The machine is Model 90 Sunbeam.

sprocket drawer claws to grip the sprocket teeth. If the cush drive assembly is dismantled before removal, it will be found that considerable difficulty will be met with the removal of the cush drive body. Easily the best method of removing the engine sprocket is with a drawer. The claw type, preferably with three jaws, is the most useful, as this can be more universally employed. They are obtainable at most accessory firms.

A Warning

The method of driving wedges or levering with tyre levers behind the sprocket and at the same time jarring the sprocket off by a sharp hammer blow applied to the end of the shaft is not advised. Even when a lead mallet or a copper drift is used, there is always the danger of loosening the mainshaft in the flywheel or bending the shaft itself. In fact, some manufacturers issue special warning against hammering the shaft under any circumstances.

In Difficult Cases

If the sprocket is particularly stiff, a blowlamp can be used to warm this until it is fairly hot, then the sprocket should be lightly tapped round the boss of the sprocket. This will loosen the sprocket on the shaft, and it should readily respond to the drawer.

6

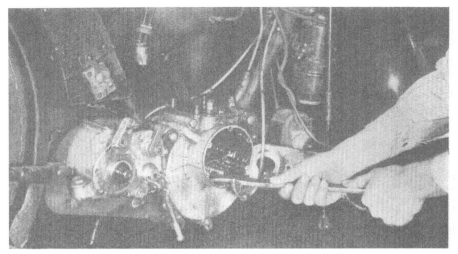

Fig. 12.—Testing a Main Bearing.

Gives a good idea how to test a main bearing during dismantling. This will be dealt with in a later article. A lever is used to lift the mainshaft against the weight of the flywheels.

How to make a Sprocket Drawer

A useful drawer can easily be made from a piece of steel about 5 inches long, $1\frac{1}{4}$ inches wide and $\frac{5}{16}$ inch thick. Drill and tap the centre of the bar $\frac{3}{8}$-inch Whitworth and fit a set screw. Cut a slot on either side of the screw $\frac{5}{16}$ inch wide. This is best done by drilling a series of holes and connecting up with a file. Two $\frac{5}{16}$-inch bolts and nuts are used to clamp the drawer in position (see Fig. 10).

Flywheel Removal

Where an external flywheel is fitted this can be removed in a similar manner, but owing to the larger circumference much heavier material should be used. Fig. 16 gives an idea how the drawer is made. Two long steel strips are riveted to a heavy steel plate which is drilled and tapped to take the centre bolt approximately $\frac{1}{2}$ inch $\times$ 20T. Two similar strips register from the other side of the flywheel and are clamped together. In very obstinate cases it may be necessary to give the pressure bolt in the centre a sharp tap with a hammer.

Dismantling Timing Gear

Remove the timing cover where the magneto is driven by gear pinions or the chain cover where chain driven. The screws in the former type sometimes give trouble, and it is advisable to use a long screwdriver. To get a good bite of the screw head this should be firmly tapped on the end of the handle, and if necesary extra leverage can be exerted with an adjustable wrench on the shank (see Fig. 11). Great care should be taken, in levering off the timing cover, not to damage the faces. Mutilated faces are impossible to rejoint satisfactorily and cause oil leaks and in consequence a dirty engine. Some designs have lugs cast on the cover to facilitate removal.

See that the Timing Pinions are Marked

Avoid disturbing the timing pinions, if at all possible, as these should be checked for marking. If these are not already marked, it should be done with a centre punch and small chisel. Where one pinion meshes with two others, one point of contact should be marked in each pinion with a dot and the other point with chisel marks. The pinions may then be removed, together with the rockers or levers, if these are fitted. Take careful note how these are positioned and the method of operation. This will save possible difficulty when reassembling.

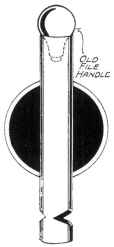

OLD FILE HANDLE

Fig. 13.—S I M P L E DEVICE FOR COMPRESSING SPRINGS TO EASY REMOVAL OF VALVE COTTERS.

Removing the Magneto

The magneto sprocket can be removed in a similar manner to that suggested for the engine sprocket. A smaller edition of the sprocket drawer can be made suitable for the magneto. Do not use a hammer on the end of the shaft or two levers as very often advised. Serious damage to the armature shaft or chaincase is usually the result. Also do not use a blowlamp on the sprocket. If heat is needed a piece of steel tubing, heated red, may be applied direct to the sprocket boss over the end of the shaft. The sprocket drawer cannot be used where a pinion is fitted, or where there is insufficient clearance between the case to take the bolt heads. Some designers provide two threaded holes, into which bolts can be screwed, thus forcing the pinion off by pressure against the case. Otherwise a pinion drawer can easily be made from a piece of mild steel approximately 1 inch wide by $\frac{3}{16}$ inch or $\frac{1}{4}$ inch thick (see Fig. 15). The method of application is self-explanatory. The hole in the centre is drilled clear to take a $\frac{5}{16}$-inch bolt, and a nut is fitted inside to take the thrust. By screwing home the bolt and holding the nut with another spanner the pinion will be forced off.

The Toughest Problem in Engine Dismantling

Removing the mainshaft pinion is very often the toughest problem of dismantling in the whole engine. Make a careful examination to ascertain the method of fitting the pinion to the shaft. This is often keyed on a tapered shaft and locked with a nut and lock washer. In some designs, Norton for instance, the lock nut has a left-hand thread. The nut is usually marked if this is the case. It will probably be found that this nut has been screwed up dead tight, in which case it will be necessary to use a good fitting box spanner with a long tommy bar. After the nut has been removed the pinion should be drawn with a similar tool as recommended for the magneto pinion. If very stubborn it may be necessary to make one of heavier material. Another type of pinion has three keyways, each giving a variation in valve timing. In this case mark the keyway to which the key has been fitted for reference when reassembling. Another type uses a tapered expanding screw. The main-shaft is parallel and slotted for a key. The centre of the shaft is bored out, tapered and finally threaded. In assembling, the pinion and key are pressed on the shaft and the taper headed screw is fitted to the centre of the shaft, expanding the end of the shaft and thus locking the pinion in position. The order of assembling is reversed for dismantling. In very early designs the pinion was screwed on the shaft, and gave con-siderable trouble to remove, unless a rather elaborate factory tool was available. This was similar to a box spanner, but had inverted teeth cut to locate with the pinion teeth, instead of the usual hexagon.

Removing a Stubborn Pinion

As a last resource the job may be tackled in the following manner. The crankcase is laid on its side, with the pinion uppermost. A tubular box spanner that will just fit is placed over the pinion and packed up with asbestos. The spanner and pinion are warmed up with a blowlamp. Molten white metal (lead would probably do) is poured into the box

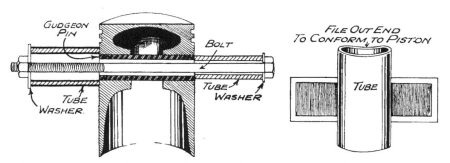

Fig. 14.—METHOD OF REMOVING GUDGEON PIN WITH BOLT AND DISTANCE PIECES.

A simple method of extracting a hollow gudgeon pin is by use of a long bolt with two pieces of brass or steel tubing. One piece with an external diameter a little smaller than the pin and the other an internal diameter a little larger than the external size of the pin. The end of the tubing in contact with the piston should be filed to conform with the side of the piston. By screwing up the nut pressure will be brought to bear on the tubing, thus forcing the pin out.

spanner, sufficient to flow between the teeth and form a hexagon from the shape of the box spanner. Warm up with the lamp to encourage the metal to flow well, then allow to cool.

Testing the Big End for Play

Test the big-end bearing for play by firmly gripping the upper half of the connecting rod with the forefinger and thumb of each hand, endeavouring to lift the rod bodily up and down. Test this in several positions of the flywheel rotation. It is often found to be the greatest on the downward thrust of rod. Should this be considered sufficient to justify attention, the crankcase can be removed from the frame. In doing so support the base with a block, thus avoiding any strain or possible damage to the threads of the anchor bolts when driving these out.

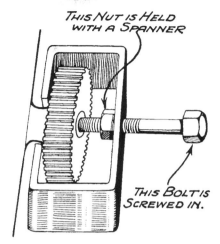

Fig. 15.—MAGNETO PINION DRAWER EASILY MADE FROM A STRIP OF MILD STEEL.

Taking Apart the Crankcase

Undo and withdraw all the crankcase bolts. The case should then come apart, leaving the flywheel assembly.

Dismantling Flywheels

Lay the flywheels on the vice with the driving side mainshaft between the jaws. On no account should the jaws be bare; always use lead clamps. Apart from the damage by causing flats and indentations, nothing looks worse than a job that has been " navvied " with vice marks and hammer dents. Use a lead or rawhide hammer or a copper drift wherever possible. Remove the crankpin-nut locking device or grub screw. The crankpin nut is sure to be done up very tightly, and it is recommended to use

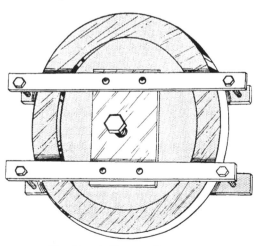

Fig. 16.—A USEFUL FLYWHEEL DRAWER.

a good-fitting box spanner. Failing this the nut may be started with a hammer and drift, but these should be avoided if possible. If the flywheels do not part readily, jar the flywheel rim with a lead or copper hammer, and this should have the desired effect. Examine the big-end bearings carefully. In most modern engines these will be the roller type, probably retained in a cage. The engine is now dismantled, with the exception of the valves and piston rings. The latter can be left until the parts are examined for wear.

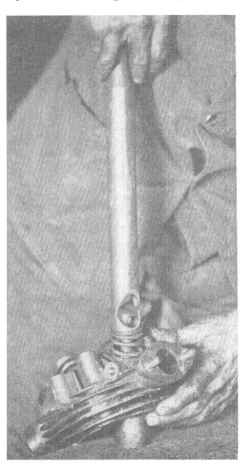

Fig. 17.—REMOVING A VALVE SPRING WITH
A HOME-MADE COMPRESSOR.

The block under the valve, to prevent this coming off the seating, will be noticed. This photograph also gives an excellent view of the split cotters exposed for removal.

Removing the Valves

Almost all makers of o.h.v. type engines supply a special tool for compressing the valve springs. In addition there are several types sold by accessory firms that can be used for most designs. " Terry " type can be recommended. A very simple tool can easily be made from a piece of steel tube. Two shallow V-shaped sections are cut out near the end of the tube, through which the cotters can be removed. A block will have to be placed under the valve head (see Figs. 13 and 17). In the case of a side-valve cylinder, the " Terry " tool is particularly suitable (see page 49, Fig. 10). Another method is that of inserting a long screwdriver blade between the fins of the cylinder and lifting up under the valve spring, compressing this to allow the cotter to be removed. A large nut should be previously placed on top of the valve, under the valve cap. The valve heads should be carefully marked before they are removed. The usual method is with a centre punch.

THE STURMEY-ARCHER GEARBOX

By T. L. Williams and S. A. Newton

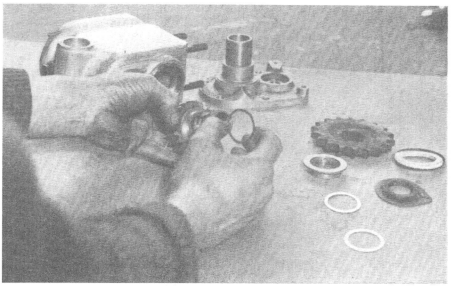

Fig. 1.—Washers used for adjusting the Double Ball Bearings which support the Main Gear Wheel.

MAINTENANCE ATTENTIONS

IT might be claimed that the gearbox should be used but not heard, but it will be appreciated that if this desirable feature is to be maintained, it will be necessary to remember its presence and regularly give that little attention which it deserves.

Lubrication

It is, for instance, essential that all the internals receive correct lubrication. The gears are not greedy in this respect, but in cases where the machine is not used for a long period, say during the winter months, it should be remembered that the oil or grease is likely to gradually drain from the upper half. The practice of running the engine slowly so as to circulate the grease for a few seconds and keep all bearings covered against

91

Fig. 2.—THE GEARS AND SHAFTS.

The dog clutches and splines have been marked to show those which engage to provide each of the three ratios.

rust is not practised as often as it should be. The fact that the box contains lubricant does not ensure that all the parts are immune from damage when such precautions are neglected.

Check Nuts Periodically

During use we must also be prepared to guard against lost nuts due to vibration. Spring washers or other locking devices are always fitted where possible, but it is also worth while going over all nuts occasionally to make sure they have not worked loose.

EXTERNAL ADJUSTMENTS

Gear Controls

Adjustments will usually be confined to the external fittings, and quite simple tests will generally indicate any need for attention. The gear control on modern machines can hardly alter of its own accord, though on older models it may be necessary to see that clamping bolts do not work loose. The moving parts of all controls also need lubrication, and vaseline or a fairly stiff grease is often preferable to oil for this purpose. It is not wise to use too much, because this will collect mud and grit, besides tending to get on to one's clothes. Do not forget the spindles round which the various levers work, nor the little swivels which connect the ends of the control rods to the levers. All these points must also be watched for wear, because as soon as any appreciable play develops, the movement which the controls should impart to the dog clutches inside the box will be lessened, and if the dogs are not pulled into full engagement, there will naturally be a tendency for them to slip out again.

When adjusting or fitting Chains

It is chiefly when the gearbox has to be moved in order to adjust the front chain that the gear control rod has to be altered in length. Assuming that the box has been slid backwards the rod must be lengthened. Remove the split pin and washer and the swivel pin which connects the gear control lever with its rod, and unscrew the connection one or two turns on the rod. If the gears are indexed internally it is easy to engage middle gear before removing this pin, and then merely adjust the top connection piece until its holes for the pin register correctly with the pin hole in the lever, so that the pin slides easily into position without any force being applied.

Adjusting Early Models

In earlier gears, where internal indexing is not adopted, the pin must be slipped in and the gears tested from the neutral position. Move the lever towards low gear, turning the back wheel to and fro all the time, and note how far it moves before you can feel the dogs just grating across each other. Then go back to neutral and move the lever towards middle gear. If the adjustment is correct the lever will move the same distance on each side before the dogs commence to engage. It is not necessary to add the washer and split pin until the correct setting has been found.

Adjusting Clutch Control

The clutch control also should be regularly checked and oiled. It is not easily possible to lubricate the Bowden wire inside its cable, but whenever a new one is fitted be sure that it is carefully greased *before* it is passed through the cable, and very little attention will afterwards be necessary. The handlebar lever must be kept free, and the security of its attachment should also be checked occasionally. Where a worm and nut operation is used at the gearbox end of the wire, the anchorage of the Bowden wire stop should always be free to swivel. This stop stud screws into the gearbox cover, but it is *not* intended that it should be screwed up tight.

Taking up Slack Cable

All Bowden cable wires are liable to stretch, and the clutch wire is probably subjected to a greater strain than the other similar controls commonly used on motor-cycles. The usual means of adjustment are provided, and it is better to rely upon the stop screw than to reset the worm lever on the worm, or to adjust the screw in the so-called direct-pull type of operating lever. It is always advisable that the lever should be as nearly vertical as possible when it takes the load of the clutch spring. With a direct-pull lever the adjusting screw should also be exactly in line with the clutch rod for best results and not pushing at an angle.

WEAR IN THE CLUTCH

We can now turn our attention to the wearing parts. First of all comes the *clutch*. Everyone will recognise that sooner or later the very act of letting in the clutch will result in the friction inserts wearing down. As this happens the outer plate will bed down nearer to the box, the clutch rod passing through the axle will become relatively too long, and the clutch control wire may possibly have to be lengthened slightly to avoid the clutch being prevented from engaging properly. This means that the tension of the clutch spring or springs will be less effective until eventually the clutch will begin to slip.

We must, however, watch that the inserts do not wear so low as to allow the metal of the plate in which they are fitted to come into contact with the plain steel plate on either side. This can sometimes happen before the slipping commences, and should therefore be guarded against.

Fig. 3.—REMOVING THE GEARBOX COVER, AND PARTING THE OILPROOF JOINT WASHER.

Fitting new Inserts

New inserts can be fitted to the plates. Sometimes corks are used and sometimes an asbestos fibre composition, of which, perhaps, the best known is Ferodo. Corks can be fitted fairly easily by hand, especially if they are first soaked in hot water. Then, when dry, lay the plate flat on a large sheet of glass paper and rub gently up and down to obtain a perfectly even surface. Ferodo or similar inserts can also be fitted by hand, but they require flattening out afterwards to secure them, and it is not easy to ensure a good flat face by hammering them out one by one. The gearbox makers have special presses for this work, and it is best to send the plates to them whenever it is possible, even if it means keeping a spare set of plates on hand.

HOW TO DISMANTLE THE CLUTCH

Instructions for dismantling clutches are given in the booklets provided free to all owners by the Sturmey-Archer Gears, Ltd., and these details are copied below.

Single-spring Clutches

First unscrew the clutch end cap, C.S. 173A. If a special spanner is not available use a hammer and a punch for this purpose. It has a right-hand thread, and must be unscrewed in an anti-clockwise direction.

Fig. 4.—Two Spanners are here being used to remove the Clutch Centre from the Mainshaft. Rather Thicker Wedges will be necessary in some Cases where a Wider Engine Chain Line is Employed.

The clutch adjuster nut is then exposed, and should be unscrewed, bearing in mind that it also has a right-hand thread. Remove clutch spring with the collar, and then the spring cup. The plates can now be withdrawn, noting particularly the direction in which the dished centre portions of these face, as they vary, and it is essential that they are replaced exactly as they were found originally. With these points carefully noted there should be no difficulty in reassembling. If the inserts are fairly thin, but otherwise in good condition, one of the washers used under the clutch adjuster nut may be removed in order to obtain additional spring tension ; also be sure the end cap is screwed up thoroughly tight.

Multi-spring Clutches

The six screws which hold the clutch springs should be unscrewed first, afterwards lifting out the springs and spring boxes. The spring box plate and the other clutch plates are then lifted apart, as described for the central spring clutches. No adjustment of the spring tension is provided, but extra strong springs are available in case of need. We do not recommend fitting these unless absolutely essential, as they are inclined to make the clutch more difficult to release.

Shock-absorber Clutches

The clutch portion can be dismantled as described for the plain type. The shock absorber may present some difficulty, as the screws holding the parts together are burred over, to prevent the lock nuts from working loose. After the four screws have been removed, the driver can be withdrawn, and the rubbers taken out of the slots in the body of the sprocket. The positions of the rubbers should be carefully noted. The solid rubbers are fitted in the driving side, and those with the small hole on the opposite side. To dismantle the bearing on the central spring type, remove the split ring and the washer behind it. The sprocket can now be taken off the centre. To remove the sprocket from the bearing in the multi-spring type, it is necessary to unscrew the six nuts on the clutch-spring studs. The small plate and the sprocket can then be removed. The sprocket bearing in the clutches is composed of loose $\frac{1}{4}$-inch diameter balls and rollers placed alternately. These should be assembled with grease.

Examine Clutch Drum Slots

If your clutch is fierce, or if you engage it suddenly, you may cause the tongues of the clutch friction plates to wear grooves in the slots of the flange in which they slide. These grooves will then prevent the plates sliding as easily and freely as they should, making it both difficult to release the clutch, and causing the re-engagement to become jerky. If the clutch sticks out, suspect this cause. The grooves can be filed away, but this is only a temporary relief, because the tongues will no longer fit snugly and the backlash allowed will cause the same wear to occur again fairly soon. You may also burr up the edges of the tongues on the plates in this way and so cause more expense.

If the Clutch is Stiff to Operate

Should stiffness develop in releasing the clutch, it is first necessary to make sure none of the strands of the control wire have broken or become rusty. In the case of the worm and nut type of control, examine the worn threads on both parts for wear, and adjust the lever on the worm to ensure that it is nearly vertical when commencing to release the plates, shortening the wire if necessary to suit, and make sure that the clutch rod inside the axle has not worn short.

Examine for Endplay

There is one gear fault that will make the clutch difficult to withdraw, namely, a floating movement of the axle from end to end of the box. Since the clutch is secured to the end of the axle, this movement has to be taken up before it is possible to start separating the clutch plates. This limits the movement of the clutch rod, which is available for releasing the clutch, and may make it impossible to obtain a perfectly free clutch. The reasons for this end movement are explained under the heading " Wear of the Gear Parts."

WEAR OF THE GEAR PARTS

How to avoid Premature Wear

It is better not to wait for some tendency of one of the gears to slip out of mesh to warn one that the gears are in need of attention. The heaviest load is applied by the weight of the clutch plus the pull of the chains on the mainshaft. This shaft passes right through the main gear wheel on all Sturmey-Archer gearboxes, and a long plain bearing occurs between these two parts. This bearing needs adequate lubrication, and it is one of the most vulnerable parts to suffer if the machine is laid up for any long period. If this happens, before taking the model on the road again, inject two or three teaspoonfuls of thin oil, and lean the machine over on the clutch side with the engine running slowly. If this thin oil will penetrate along the oil grooves on the axle, the thicker lubricant recommended for general use will follow later, but if the bearing is once allowed to become dry, the ordinary grease in the box will not work its way along. The only remedy then is to completely dismantle everything and smear the axle with grease before reassembling.

Testing Main Bearing

When the axle wears thinner or the main gear-wheel bore wears larger, you will be able to move the clutch up and down to the extent of the play allowed. But in this test it must also be remembered that if the main gear wheel is slack in its own bearings, the clutch can be lifted to this extent over and above the play existing in the plain bearing. The main gear-wheel bearings consist of a double cup and cone arrangement, and the two cones on the gear wheel are renewable. Also a few thin adjusting washers are used between them, so that if the bearing surfaces remain in good condition, you can remove these washers one at a time, so bringing the cones very slightly closer together to adjust the bearing exactly. This, of course, involves completely dismantling everything, and is probably a job the average amateur will prefer to place in practical hands, but it should never be neglected, as it is likely to cause more serious trouble if allowed to develop.

Result of Worn Main Bearings

The up-and-down movement of the clutch is unlikely to cause any running troubles unless it is excessive. If, however, it is due to slackness in the main gear-wheel bearings, it will be

Fig. 5.—The Kick-starter Parts, with the Pawl which revolves the Low Gear Wheel just disengaged from the Cam, which depresses it when the Crank returns to Rest. The Lower "Cam" is the Stop which prevents the Crank and Axle from going back too far and letting the Pawl into engagement again.

accompanied by in-and-out movement on both sprockets. This implies movement of the high gear dogs, and is likely to cause some difficulty in engaging top gear. It also allows the axle to slide to the same extent, and this affects the middle gear and the clutch operation.

Endplay—Cause and Effect

Between the main gear wheel and the splines on the axle a thrust washer is fitted. This slips over a small peg in the axle, and so cannot revolve round the axle. It takes the weight of the clutch spring whenever the clutch is held out, and it will in time wear thin. Then the axle has a further chance to move sideways, helping the middle gear to slip out, and again interfering with the clutch withdrawal. Whilst the wear is only slight, an extra washer may be inserted between the ball bearing and the clutch nut in the gearbox cover. When the clutch nut is screwed up again the ball bearing will be forced inwards a little and take up this slackness. There should be only a just perceptible movement, but we must guard against over-adjustment, which would cause overload of the main gear-wheel bearings. This is harmful, of course.

Carefully Examine

For the rest we can only test the shafts for straightness and look for wear by rounding of the various dog clutches. It is to be understood that the splines on both shafts are included in this term, and we also include the splines along the internal bore of both sliding pinions. We indicate below the dog clutches involved in the case of each gear, and then we must describe how to dismantle the box for inspection.

Top Gear.—Main gear wheel and outer dogs on axle sliding pinion.

Middle Gear.—Inner splines on both sliding pinions and the splines on both shafts.

Low Gear.—Outer dogs on layshaft sliding pinion and slots in kick-starter wheel.

In the case of any broken teeth, always suspect that the shafts may be bent, and see that they are tested and proved straight before using them again. Also if teeth on only one wheel have broken, be very careful to examine the pinion which meshes with those teeth, and make quite sure that it is safe to use it again before attempting to do so.

TO DISMANTLE THE BOX

First disconnect the clutch control wire, and if the gear control operates through the gearbox cover, disconnect the control rod at its lower end. Then remove the cover nuts and gently pull off the cover plate. There are spring washers over each cover stud, so be careful not to lose these. Also do not use a screwdriver or anything similar to part the joint, or oil will leak at this point when reassembled. If the plate sticks, it can usually be removed by one or two light blows with a mallet on the back of the kick-starter crank. The low-gear pinion can be pulled off the mainshaft (it is a push fit over the splined end), and then the complete layshaft and pinions, together with the sliding gear plate and the axle sliding pinion can be lifted out. It may be needless to remove the fork, but if desired the nut which locks the rocking shaft lever should now be unscrewed and the lever withdrawn. Unscrew the bush from the opposite side of the box and knock out the spindle. Always hold a piece of brass or hard wood against threaded parts to prevent damage to the threads when knocking out.

Fig. 6.—How the Lay Shaft and both Sliding Pinions are fitted into Position together. Note how the Pegs on the Sliding Gearplate are being engaged with the Slots in the Operating Fork.

Now turn to the clutch, and dismantle according to instructions already given. To remove the clutch centre from the axle, insert two steel wedges behind it, between that part and the rear drive sprocket. A couple of screwdrivers will do. Tap these in until wedged. Remove the nut and lock washer from the axle. Then hold a piece of brass or hard wood against the axle end, and give one or two sharp blows with a hammer. The brass is merely to protect the screw thread. If this does not loosen the centre, tap in the wedges a little tighter and try again. You can then

7

remove the screws, securing the locking plate on the rear-drive sprocket, and unscrew the sprocket lock nut. Pull off the sprocket, which is a push fit over six splines, and knock the main gear wheel into the shell. In doing this you will release twenty balls $\frac{1}{4}$ inch in diameter from each side of the ball cup in the shell, so be careful not to lose these.

The Kick-starter Parts

First examine the ratchet teeth inside the kick-starter wheel, which is also the low-gear wheel on the layshaft. Then look at the nose of the pawl in the kick-starter axle. It will be best to remove the crank and drop the kick-starter axle from the gearbox cover for examination. It will then be possible to make sure that the pawl plunger and spring are working properly, and that the pin on which the pawl swivels is not broken. If any damage is revealed here, see also that the walls of the kick-starter axle on each side of the pawl are not cracked. Also see that the cam in the box cover depresses the pawl correctly when the kick-starter axle is revolved in the cover.

Reassembling

Fit up the main gear wheel first after setting one row of balls in grease. Set up the other row of balls on their cone, and slip this into position, not forgetting the adjusting washers that go between the cones. Fix the rear drive sprocket and tighten up its lock nut. Then test to see that the main bearings are correctly adjusted and revolve freely but with no shake. If there is shake you must remove one of the washers from between the cones so that the cones can come closer together.

Now fit up the sliding gear fork. Then smear the axle with grease, pass it through the main gear wheel (with thrust washer in position, of course) and assemble the clutch.

The layshaft and its sliding pinion, assembled with the sliding gear plate and axle sliding pinion, are next fitted as one unit, and by holding the end of the layshaft in one hand and the rocking-shaft lever in the other, you can move the fork over to receive the sliding gear plate correctly, and drop all these parts into position together. There is now only the low-gear pinion to push on the end of the mainshaft and the kick-starter wheel to add. Reassemble the kick-starter axle and crank to the box cover, and these should fall into position without any straining.

Early Models—Important Note

One last word regarding the kick-starter. In older models an external stop spring is relied upon to prevent the pawl passing the cam which depresses it. This spring may give, if subject to much backfiring, and if it does the pawl comes into action again and forces the crank forwards, sometimes breaking a footboard. Therefore keep a watchful eye on this spring, and do not omit to renew it if necessary.

REPAIRS AND ADJUSTMENTS TO THE RALEIGH ENGINE

By T. L. WILLIAMS and B. F. C. FELLOWES

THE ordinary routine work of decarbonising being dealt with elsewhere, we will assume that the engine is to be removed from the frame for complete dismantling and overhaul as necessary.

Dismantling

The machine should be stood on its rear stand, and the front wheel wedged by a block to prevent any possibility of the machine moving in a forward direction. Removal of all extraneous fittings, such as petrol pipes and carburetter, exhaust pipe or pipes in the case of the twin port machine, magneto driving chain, engine chain, chaincase, footrests, and sparking plug, etc., is a simple matter, and the valve lifter mechanism should then be removed. This latter is quite simple in all cases, needing no explanation.

Removing Outside Type Flywheel

Most of the earlier Raleigh models were fitted with an outside flywheel, and this must be removed before the engine plate bolts can be withdrawn. On $2\frac{3}{4}$-h.p. models a flywheel cap is fitted, having a left-hand thread. This should be unscrewed, when will be seen the crankshaft or flywheel nut lock plate. Unbend this, and then unscrew the nut until it protrudes a short distance over the end of the shaft. Then replace the cap, which should be screwed up against the flywheel nut by means of the special "Cee" spanner provided in the standard Raleigh tool kit. A few light taps with a wooden mallet will suffice to cause the flywheel to come adrift from the taper shaft. It should here be noted that a key is not fitted, the two perfectly ground tapers being quite sufficient to firmly hold the flywheel.

The Lightweight Model Flywheel

The procedure for $2\frac{1}{4}$-h.p. models is a little different. No flywheel cap is fitted, and after bending back the lock washer as described for $2\frac{3}{4}$-h.p. models, remove the nut and then pack suitable wedges (wood for preference) between the back of the flywheel rim and engine plates. A few taps on the end of the shaft, again with a wooden mallet, will then free the wheel.

How to remove the Sprocket

Before actual removal of the flywheel it would be as well to inspect the engine sprocket. If worn, the teeth will be hook shaped, and replace-

Fig. 1.—Binding back the Flywheel Nut Lock Plate.

ment necessary. The sprocket is screwed to a boss on the flywheel by a right-hand thread. Lightly tap the sprocket round, by means of a hammer and a copper drift if available, otherwise a short piece of hardwood will serve.

Dealing with Cylinder Trouble

The flywheel, in the case of this type of engine, having been taken off, the bolts can next be removed, and the engine dropped out of the frame. Hold the engine in the vice by means of the crankcase bosses, and remove the cylinder. It may be that slight score marks will be felt rather than seen. If these are only slight, " lapping " out will most probably suffice to effect their removal. The best method of doing this is to make a wooden " connecting rod " with a hole in the " small end " to take the gudgeon pin. Hold the cylinder firmly in the vice by means of the flange, and

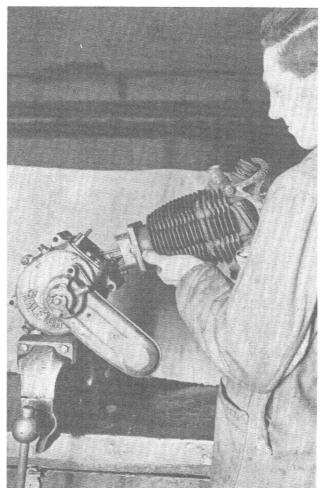

Fig. 2.—HOLD THE ENGINE IN THE VICE BY MEANS OF THE CRANKCASE BOSSES AND REMOVE THE CYLINDER.

then smear the rings and cylinder bore with a mixture of metal polish and paraffin. If available, an old piston should be used for this job, though not absolutely necessary. Work the piston up and down in the cylinder bore, at the same time imparting a twisting motion (Fig. 3). The process should be continued until the marks can be felt to have disappeared, and a set of new rings should then be fitted. The method of fitting these is described in another section, but in the case of Raleigh machines, the correct gap is, on standard machines ·005 inch, and on sports ·015 inch. When the new rings have been fitted the piston should again be "lapped in" for a few minutes. Incidentally, this same process should always be followed when fitting an entirely new piston.

Valve Guides

The valves and valve guides should next receive treatment, the inlet valve guide in particular being examined for, and replaced in the event of, wear, because otherwise this will cause a bad air leakage, making starting extremely difficult.

Timing Gear

Before removing the timing cover, test the timing gear for "back lash," bearing the result in mind when the cam and rocker gear are under examination at a later stage.

Next remove the timing cover, held by cheese-headed screws, and note whether the cam and rockers have worn. This is not likely until many thousands of miles have been covered, but if so will be obvious by the appearance of "flats." Should these "flats" be only slight, they may be "rubbed" down by means of an oilstone. Grinding should not be attempted, as the rockers are case hardened.

Before splitting the crankcase, difficulty may be experienced in withdrawing the crankshaft pinion. A lock washer is used to secure the nut, and after its removal a pulley drawer, if available, should be employed to extract the pinion. If not available, two tyre levers will be found as good a means as any for accomplishing this (Fig. 5).

Examine Main Bearings

Before actually splitting the crankcase test the mainshaft for sideplay by pulling on the engine sprocket. No up-and-down play is permissible, but slight endplay, not exceeding $\frac{1}{32}$ inch, may be allowed. The races themselves should also be examined, and if worn, replaced. Wear on these races will be felt if they are moved by the two thumbs while the case is on the bench.

Fitting New Main Bearings

Removal of the races sometimes presents difficulty to the amateur. Immerse, for a few moments, the half case from which it is desired to remove the race in water which has nearly reached boiling-point. This will cause the case to expand, and a light tap of the case on to the wooden bench will allow the bearing to drop out. The same process may be followed when fitting a new race.

The difficulty likely to arise in connection with the stripping down and rebuilding of the big-end bearing is the removal, and later the tightening up, of the crankpin nut. Of the two, the timing side nut will offer the least resistance.

Fitting Big-end Bearings

On removal of the nut, gently tap the shaft with a rawhide mallet, which will cause the shaft to then spring off the crankpin taper. The connecting rod can then be withdrawn, and the work of fitting new rollers, if required, proceeded with. The method of doing this is to pack the

Fig. 3.—WORK THE PISTON UP AND DOWN IN THE CYLINDER BORE.

crankpin with grease, setting the rollers round the pin in the same way as the balls are set in an ordinary hub bearing.

Factory Method

At the Raleigh Works the flywheels are assembled on " Vee " blocks, and the use of an " Ames " dial gauge, recording to an accuracy of half a thousandth part of an inch, ensures them running absolutely true (Fig. 8). Also, for finally locking up, a special box spanner and long tommy bar is used, and for these two reasons the amateur at least will be well advised to despatch the complete crankshaft assembly to works for overhaul when required.

An Alternative

The alternative method of lining up the flywheels is to first tighten up the crankpin nut until the flywheels are tightly held, and then place the shafts between lathe centres. They can then be rotated by means of the connecting rod, and any eccentricity will be observed from the way in which they run. At each sight, they must be removed from the lathe and tapped in the correct direction and then again tested. This must be repeated until perfect alignment is achieved. It will be seen that absolute truth is essential on this particular job, and the greatest care must be

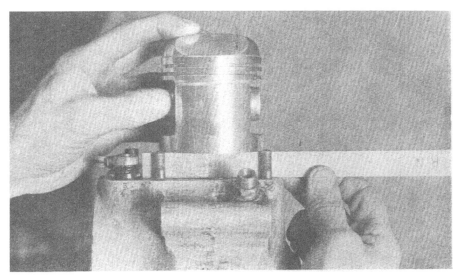

Fig. 4.—How to detect Bad Alignment of the Connecting Rod.

Lay a steel straightedge across the crankcase cylinder faces as shown above, then rotate the engine until on the down stroke the piston skirt meets the straightedge. If the connecting rod is not in line the edge of the piston will not coincide with the straightedge. If this is the case the connecting rod must be carefully aligned, using a cranking iron.

taken when finally tightening up the crankpin nut that alignment is not altered.

An Important Reminder

The method of heating the crankcase by immersion in hot water for the purpose of fitting new mainshaft races has already been dealt with, but it would perhaps be as well to give here a reminder of the importance of not omitting to fit the bearing retaining ring or rings which fit in grooves cut in the shafts. On some Raleigh models there is a retaining ring for both races, on others for the timing side race only, and in the case of the " MJ " and " MO " models neither race is so fitted, but this is obvious by the absence of the grooves.

If it should be necessary to fit a new bush to the little-end bearing of the connecting rod the old bush should be drawn out and the replacement pressed in.   Any attempt to knock out the old bush will almost be certain to cause the new bearing to be out of line, and may even result in bending the connecting rod.

To withdraw the bush, obtain an ordinary hexagon-headed bolt and nut, say ½ inch in diameter and about 4 inches long, a washer just slightly less than the outside diameter of the bush, and a sleeve or short length of tubing just slightly larger than the bush. The washer should then be slipped over the bolt, and the latter inserted through the bush. Next fit the sleeve along the remainder of the bolt, and by tightening up the nut against a second washer the bush will be withdrawn from the rod through the sleeve. Obviously a reversal of the operation will allow the new bush to be pressed into place in exactly the same way.

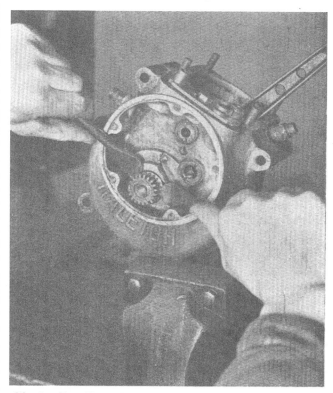

Fig. 5.—Two Tyre Levers may be used to withdraw the Crankshaft Pinion.

Incidentally, when this has been done, do not forget to drill the oil hole in the bush, in line with the hole in the connecting rod itself.   (See also Fig. 9, p. 114.)

Check the Connecting Rod

A frequent cause of excessive piston wear and seizure is connecting rod mal-alignment, which can easily be checked. With the cylinder removed, lay a steel straightedge across the crankcase cylinder faces, and then rotate the engine until on the down stroke the piston skirt meets the straightedge. If the connecting rod is not in line, this will be immediately apparent. A cranking iron can be used to bend the rod in the desired direction ; naturally, great care must be exercised. (See Fig. 4, p. 108.)

Valve Thimbles

On the earlier types of Raleigh 348-c.c. and 496-c.c. twin-port o.h.v. engines, case-hardened steel thimbles were fitted to the ends of the valve stems to prevent wear. Later, this was discontinued and a slightly different design of overhead rocker employed. It will be seen, therefore, that where engines have left works with the new type rocker without the thimbles, these must not afterwards be fitted.

SEEKING THOSE EXTRA M.P.H.—SPECIAL TUNING HINTS

As is well known, the Raleigh Company list a very fast racing machine known as the 350-c.c. T.T. Replica. As the name implies, this machine is in all respects an exact replica of those which have competed so successfully in numerous important races during the last two years or more. To many, however, the original cost of such a machine is prohibitive, but consolation may be taken in the fact that owners of any of the o.h.v. types can obtain a few miles per hour more from their machines by following carefully the hints here given.

Attention to the Ports

First of all, the cylinder head and valve ports must be carefully polished, the inlet valve and around the plug hole in particular. This is rather a tedious operation except where facilities exist for the job to be done by means of a small emery wheel attached to a flexible shaft, which of course is the method adopted by the makers. A 6-inch half-round file should be obtained, and after softening bent to a shape which will permit of easy working through the valve ports and inside the head. Before rehardening make sure that the bend is sufficient or, on the other hand, not too steep to permit of easy handling.

Factory Assistance

The head must be carefully held in the vice and the job can then be commenced in earnest. Take the greatest care not to damage the valve seatings, and when sufficient material has been removed finish off with emery paper. This is a job which can be very efficiently carried out by the Raleigh Cycle Co., Ltd., at the modest cost of 7s. 6d. only, and for this reason it is doubtful whether the trouble to the private owner is really worth while.

Now the Piston

The piston should next be dealt with. Any high spots should be very carefully removed by means of a fine Swiss file—note, not emery paper. These spots, if present, will be found as bright areas standing out quite boldly from the usual greyness of the piston. Make sure also that the piston has sufficient clearance, especially on the four sharp edges and just above the rings. The rings themselves should be lapped into the cylinder as previously described, and of course correctly gapped. In this connection, do not remove one of the rings unless the event in which the machine is competing is a sprint race of a few hundred yards only. Naturally, the valves must be given special attention and make perfect contact on their seatings, and, moreover, the stems must be quite free in their guides. A really good plug is essential for high-speed work, the Lodge type H.45 being particularly suitable.

If the Compression Plate is Removed

The compression plate underneath the cylinder flange should be

Fig. 6.—A Light Tap of the Case on to the Bench will allow the Bearing to Drop Out.

removed, and the engine must then be run on a petrol-benzol mixture and a larger jet fitted to the carburetter to suit the changed conditions.

Do not Forget

It should here be noted that when the plate is removed the piston will travel farther up the cylinder barrel. A ridge of hard carbon will most likely have formed at the extreme top of the barrel, where the piston crown originally came to, and this must be removed, as otherwise the piston, travelling higher, will strike this hard ridge, and broken piston rings will result.

H.C. Pistons

Should a still higher compression ratio be needed, the manufacturers will supply a special piston and rings, which will raise the compression ratio, from, in the case of the 500-c.c. machine, 5·75 to 1 to 8 to 1, and the 350-c.c. machine from 5·7 to 1 to 7·75 to 1. For the 500-c.c. machine the piston in question is known as MR. 208 and piston rings MR. 209, and for the 350-c.c. machine piston MS. 345 and piston rings MS. 348. With either of these pistons fitted it is necessary to employ an alcohol fuel such as P.M.S. 2 or R.D. 1, and the carburetter must be tuned to suit. Fit a ·113 needle jet when either of the above fuels are used, and for P.M.S. 2 a size 300–325 jet, and with R.D. 1 a size 350–375 jet. Owing to alcohol fuels showing a great variation, the correct jet size can only be determined by trial and error.

Special Springs

A most important point to bear in mind when the sports piston is fitted is that stronger valve springs will be required, and in fact they

Fig. 7.—PACK THE CRANKPIN WITH GREASE.

Fig. 8.—Testing the Flywheel Assembly by Means of a Dial Gauge.
An interesting workshop process, but not a job for the amateur.

should be changed fairly frequently, as they lose their tension after a time. When ordering, the numbers of these springs are MS. 373 and MS. 374 inner and outer respectively.

More Advance

The ignition timing will require a different setting, which again will best be found by experiment on the road. This, however, will be somewhere in the region of 40° of advance before top dead centre. After arriving at, and making the final setting, see that the adjustment of the magneto driving chain is normal, because if this is allowed to slacken off it will retard the ignition and, in addition, cause the engine to run hot.

General Hints

Do not make the mistake of giving all the attention to the engine only. The front forks and fork shock-absorber adjustment must be just right for the rider's weight. Tyre pressures must be as recommended by the manufacturers, and in order to obtain perfect steering the wheels must be in absolute alignment. This can be checked by laying a long straightedge, or even a piece of tightly stretched string, alongside both wheels, and then adjusting until contact is made by the rims at the four points.

Chains which are too tight will not only cause excessive wear on the sprockets and impose an unfair strain on the engine and gearbox bearings, but will definitely cause a decrease in the maximum speed of the machine. Therefore, err on the side of slackness. The wheel bearings themselves must be absolutely free, and both brakes should be adjusted so that there is no possibility of them binding.

Particularly if the event to be entered is over a long distance, adjust the handlebars, footrests and saddle, so that the rider feels really " at home." This is most important, as besides minimising physical fatigue, a correct riding position will cause the machine to be faster, due to lessened wind resistance, and even more important, will give the rider a sense of perfect security and control.

For normal fast road work the standard gear ratios are best. Even when running downhill a higher gear is of no advantage, but in stripped condition, and when fitted with lighter tyres and wheels, the engine will undoubtedly pull a higher gear, which can be brought about by fitting a one-, or perhaps two-tooth larger engine sprocket.

Fig. 9.—The Bush being withdrawn from the Rod through the Sleeve.

For touring work a mineral oil will be found most suitable, but for racing use a castor base lubricant, although this will necessitate more frequent decarbonisation. The Raleigh lubrication system, forks, frames and cycle parts are dealt with later in the appropriate sections.

SPECIAL HINTS ON SCOTT ENGINES

By J. H. KELLY (*Scott Motors Ltd.*)

Fig. 1.—REMOVING THE CRANKPIN SCREW.
Note how the crankcase door flange is machined away to allow for crankpin screw removal.

TAKING DOWN A SCOTT ENGINE

FIRST, a timely warning : DON'T TAKE OFF THE WATERCOOLED HEAD FOR DECARBONISING—this is only a water jacket, and is distinct from the cylinder itself.

Removing the Cylinders

Drain water from radiator, take out plugs, radiator (gently please !), remove silencer, transfer covers, cylinder holding-down bolts, carburetter on Supers only (not essential, but allows more room), and on Supers right-hand exhaust port cover. Then lift off the cylinders.

If these are tight, replace plugs, engage gear, open throttle and turn

Fig. 2.—Removing Piston and Rod complete from Crankcase.
Note the right hand tilts the rod and the left hand turns flywheel backwards, thus drawing
crankpin bush away from con rod.

back wheel *slowly*, until block moves up from the crankcase against compression.

Crankcase Doors

Having removed crankcase doors (on late Flyers and Replicas these must be removed *before* cylinder bolts can be taken out), remove crankpin screws, stamped right- and left-hand respectively, by using door strap as screwdriver. If these are tight, tap end of strap whilst in screw slot ; failing that, tap gently with hammer and light punch. (On Supers and Flyers it will be noted that the crankcase door flange is machined away at one point to allow for removal of screw : it will only come away at this point—don't force.)

Pistons and Con Rods—Removal

Take out big-end rollers (count them in your hand—12 each side), then turn flywheel to top of stroke—tilt con rod sideways, turn flywheel back slightly—i.e. taking crankpin bush " out of the con rod," piston and con rod come out together nicely.

All gudgeons (except very old type, split-pinned or lock ringed) tap out from the inside (i.e. flywheel side), and if piston bosses are at all worn, oversize gudgeons *must* be fitted, otherwise the old gudgeons will eventually float out, with unhappy results to the cylinder walls. (*Note.*—Oversize gudgeons, $\frac{12}{1000}$ in oversize, are supplied by works and depot.)

Pistons and Con Rods—Adjustment and Repairs

If pistons show signs of having seized, ease off *lightly* with a very fine file, and if cylinders are marked, lap out with crocus powder and oil, but extreme care must be taken to ensure that the cylinders are washed perfectly free of powder afterwards. Don't use your own pistons for this job—beg, borrow, or steal an old one.

When trying pistons and rings in cylinders, put a small wad of paper in the head first, as in some cases it is possible to jam the piston rings if the piston is pushed too far up into the head.

If the rings show more than $\frac{10}{1000}$ gap, fit new ones (using only genuine Scott rings for the job: cheap rings mean loss of efficiency, and are false economy, anyhow).

Fig. 3.—REMOVING RIGHT-HAND CRANK.

Note centre bolt is slackened off a few turns, and a sharp blow drives out crank. WARNING: support crankcase on a block of wood first, and see that the crankpin bush on the under side registers with the crankcase cut away—otherwise the flange may get broken when the crank drops out.

Genuine Scott rings are supplied slightly oversize (circumference), and it may be necessary to file slightly to fit (incidentally, radial depth and width are dead right on these rings) inspect your gaps through the ports ;

8

Fig. 4.—GRINDING IN PACKING GLANDS ON SCOTT ENGINE BEFORE REASSEMBLY.
The method is described in detail on page 123.

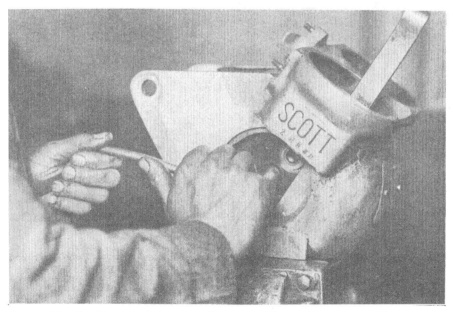

Fig. 5.—UNDOING LEFT-HAND THREADED NUT OF CRANKSHAFT BOLT.
Lay a tyre lever or strip of metal (NOT SHARP EDGES, PLEASE ! !) in crankcase as shown,
and the crank pin bush will rest on it whilst nut is being slackened off.

and remember that old engines wear more at the middle than at the bottom of the stroke, and a ring tight at the bottom may be just right at the top ; make due allowance for this, and fit each ring separately.

Clean ring grooves thoroughly, and roll rings round piston ; don't have any " sticky " spots (a free ring is very necessary for a two-stroke and one tight ring spoils the whole performance), and if an old ring has been badly seized in, chamfer the piston ring groove edge very slightly.

Refitting Rings for Fast Work

For "fast" work rings should be fitted with a very small gap and lapped in with jewellers' rouge and oil. The same warning *re* cleaning your pistons and cylinders applies here.

Engines should be run carefully for fifty miles (a little oil in the petrol is advisable), and if fitted for fast work, one hundred miles.

Use an ordinary penknife or a Woolworth's scout-knife for removing carbon, clean all ports thoroughly, polish your pistons vigor-

Fig. 6.—BUILDING UP CRANKSHAFT.

After the crank bolt has been screwed up, each crank should be driven into the flywheel, using a hammer and tubular punch.

ously *on the top only* with metal polish (this will render your next decoke easier), and clean out the oil grooves, but do not polish the sides of the pistons.

Reassembling Pistons and Con Rods

When replacing con rods, put these back correctly. It is generally assumed that, as long as the small-end bush fixing screw is uppermost, all is well, but it isn't.

A small centre-punch mark will be seen on the side of the rod, at the

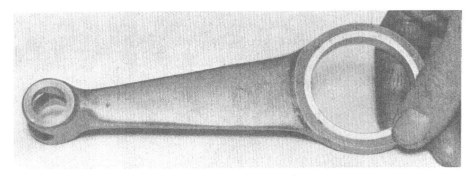

Fig. 7.—SHOWING CENTRE-PUNCH MARK ON CON ROD.
This side faces flywheel.

top, near the small end, and this should face the flywheel ; keep each rod to its own side of the engine, as they come out.

Watercooled Head

If this leaks badly, remove two locking rings and lift off the head ; clean the surfaces carefully, fit new rubber and c/a washers ; use Hermetite or Metalastine, allow to get tacky before putting on the head, tighten the head down evenly and *gently* (remember the head is very thin), and allow to stand for a few hours before filling with water.

It will be found that the head can be tightened a little more after a day or so's running.

Did you know this ?

The London Depot of Scott Motors, Ltd., will be pleased to lend a special spanner for these head nuts against a deposit of 10*s.* ; no charge is made for use and deposit is returned in full.   The same facility is given in the case of a half-compression locking-ring tool, the deposit here being 5*s.*

Joints

Always use new packings, these are quite cheap.

All joints should be fitted dry, except base linen rings, on which you may use either seccotine or oil.   Trim up transfer and induction washers to the ports, to ensure an even flow of gas.

Gauzes

These are fitted to most 596 engines and the early 486 and 532 models, but a little more speed and acceleration may be gained by their removal. If the engine spits badly with the gauzes out, replace them immediately.

Cylinder Bolts

When tightening down the cylinder holding-down bolts, do these diagonally ; this relieves the " last bolt " of undue strain.

A Warning—leave the Skirts alone

Many Scott owners, no doubt intrigued by the usual press photos and descriptions of T.T. Scotts, or inspired by those weird and wonderful tuning hints so freely broadcast, have rushed blindly into the practice of cutting away the cylinder skirts below the cylinder transfer ports in order to gain a little more speed and acceleration.

Whilst it is more than likely that this end has been attained, the slow running has been practically destroyed—a little thought will explain why!

Now the T.T. Replica, of course, *is* cut away, BUT *the inlet and exhaust ports are altered accordingly* to balance up for the slow running. This part of the business is never mentioned by the " tuning expert."

Never meddle with these dangerous experiments ; remember the Scott Works and the Depot are always only too willing to give advice on such points : they will be delighted to help you get the best out of your Scott.

HOW TO TAKE SCOTT ENGINE OUT OF FRAME

Having attended to the cylinders and pistons, it now remains to get the balance of the engine out of the frame, as follows :

Remove engine chains, (engine and/or magneto), four bottom $\frac{3}{8}$-inch engine bolts and large top bolt, and lift assembly from frame.

In the Case of " Flyer " Models

Support crankcase with box or petrol can, remove chains, take out carburetter slides, disconnect clutch wire, remove three main engine bolts, taking out the *top* one last.

For 1928–31 Flyers take out *front* bolt first and

Fig. 8.—CORRECT WAY TO REPLACE FLYWHEEL.
Note fingers rest naturally in deep rim of flywheel.

remove front stand ; when reassembling, put this bolt back first, *without* stand and washers, and after replacing other two bolts, take out front one again and replace stand and washers at your ease.   This saves a lot of " juggling " with front stand.

REPLACING ENGINES (COMPLETE) IN FRAME

Super will go back into frame quite comfortably if the right-hand exhaust port cover is left off.

"Flyer" Models

These should be put in upside down and swung up into position (see Fig. 10), fitting front bolt (only) first (see note *re* 1928–31 Flyers above).

Incidentally, it is worth while taking out the gearbox at the same time on these models, as on removal of two gear tray bolts and nuts, sprocket housing complete, two underneath nuts to gearbox studs, the tray can be swung downwards and the whole gearbox dropped through the frame—an extra five minutes' work !   This will also save discon-

Fig. 9.—It is possible to examine the Piston Ring Gap through Transfer Port.

necting the gear chain, which will come out with the engine.

A Note on the Threespeed Super

In this particular job it is far simpler and easier to remove engine and gearbox on the undertray in one unit—but don't forget to remove the clutch wire first—so easily forgotten !

DISMANTLING CRANKSHAFT

A delicate job, but quite straightforward. Proceed as follows : unscrew LEFT-hand nut in centre of right-hand crank, undo bolt on left-hand side a few turns (right-hand thread), a smart blow on the bolt head will dislodge crank ; bolt can then be unscrewed, releasing right-hand crank and rollers. (COUNT THEM—SUPERS 13, and FLYERS 15.)

The left-hand crank can then be removed by a steel bar passed through the flywheel, giving it a smart blow.

Take great care in replacing cranks ; a little grease (vaseline) will hold the rollers in position (bed these down on the bearing by passing a piece of string round the outside of rollers, when in position, and tighten), replace packing gland (after grinding this in with a little *fine* valve-grinding paste or knife-powder, see Fig. 4) and be sure that the tongue of this engages with the keyway in the flywheel.

After the crank bolt is screwed up, each crank should be driven into the flywheel, using a hammer and tubular punch (three sharp blows only).

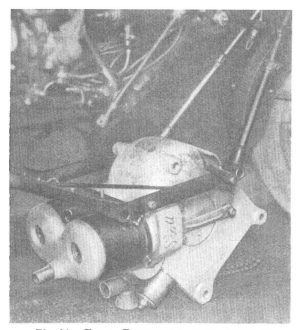

Fig. 10.—FLYER ENGINE READY TO SWING UP INTO FRAME.

Warning

Whenever hammering up a crank, the other one *must* be in position first and a solid mass brought to bear up against it, so that the force of the blow is not transferred to the crankcase cup.

Each crank must be knocked up in turn and crank bolt tightened a little, and cranks MUST be driven up solid to flywheel, otherwise the flywheel key may shear.

Always use a new crankshaft bolt and nut, as these tend to " stretch," and left-hand thread is invariably damaged.

When tightening up bolt and nut, don't overdo it ; the left-hand nut may need to be thinned down to clear the large hole roller plate. See that the latter seats firmly on the crank, then check that it really clears the nut ; rivet the nut over lightly to prevent working loose.

When replacing flywheel, see that this is put back right, i.e. the fingers of the right hand fall naturally into the groove of the rim. *Flyers*, the thin sprocket will be on your right (magneto chain drive).

The sprockets usually last for years, but can be replaced for a few shillings, and are only riveted on to the flywheel. (20-tooth only supplied.)

If main bearings or cups are worn, the cranks and crankcase must be returned to the WORKS for new parts to be fitted, as these are not supplied separately.

Big Ends

If your bushes or rollers show signs of pitting or " scaling " they should be replaced. (Works and London depot will rebush or exchange rods and cranks for you at a reasonable charge.)

Don't waste your time or money on oversize rollers—rebushing is not expensive, and the Scott engine, as an engineering job, surely deserves a better fate than faking up big ends ! ! When you realise that explosion force does not wear the bushes *evenly*, you *must* see that the oversize rollers are altogether wrong ! !

GENERAL NOTES ON SCOTT ENGINES

Air Leaks

These can generally be found by squirting petrol around the various joints ; pulling off each plug lead separately will instantly show which cylinder is weak, although a blown carburetter (induction pipe) washer *may* lead you badly astray (check this first) !

Intermittent firing or cutting out on one side may be due to cracked pick-ups (H.T.), but more elusive is the burnt contact-breaker points, or loosening of same ; early Lucas Magdynos are peculiarly sensitive on these points. Too wide a gap at the plug or magneto points is another cause.

Plugs for Scott Engines

A very debatable point this ! but a just golden rule. *If you are satisfied with your present plugs,* DON'T *change, stick to that type.* Apart from this, here are the recommended types.

GENERAL AND TOURING

Champion No. 13 (for 1929–31 Flyers, No. 7).

FAST TOURING

K.L.G. H.S. 3.
Lodge H.H. 1.
Champion Aero A (for 1927–8 Flyers and T.T. Replicas only).

Fig. 11.—Lifting Super Engine out of Frame.

Fig. 12.—SHOWING REMOVAL OF KICK-STARTER DEVICE.
Lifting gear with screwdriver and sliding off device.

RACING

K.L.G. 268 and Champion Aero A.

Warning

Plugs with a longer reach than ¾ inch must not be used ; damage to pistons is the penalty !

Timing

Take out plug, set piston at top of stroke, retard ignition lever fully, set contact-breaker points just fully opened. If you have timed off the wrong cylinder, this will be denoted by a backfire in the silencer ; it is then necessary to change over the plug leads.

Oil

Use Castrol XXL (or " runners up " Castrol XL, Duckhams' Adcol R.R.).

Petrol

Any good brand of No. 1 (OR BETTER STILL 50 per cent. petrol to 50 per cent. pure benzole). For T.T. Replicas, ethyl.

Decoke new engines, 1,500 miles ; afterwards, 2,000 to 4,000 miles, according to model.

Scott Radiator

Perished hoses and rubber pads for bolts should be renewed, and in the event of a new hose weeping, a few turns of insulation tape round the brass water pipes will cure this.

The water system should be flushed out occasionally with warm water and soda to remove any deposit.

To prevent freezing in cold weather add about a pint and a quarter of ordinary commercial glycerine to the radiator water. If you cannot get glycerine, empty the radiator by the drain tap in the cylinder, but make sure that it *is* empty, as if there is a rust deposit at the cylinder end it is quite likely that it will block up the drain tap.

For a small honeycomb leak, stop this up with a piece of chewing gum (*after* you have chewed it !)—this is quite a good tip, as you can get this anywhere on the road, where you probably could not get Plasticine. Have the leak repaired as soon as possible (corrosion sets in very quickly and spreads) by a skilled radiator repair man. DON'T TACKLE IT YOUR-SELF.

Silencers for Scott Machines

The Howarth silencer, fitted to Flyers, etc., is very prone to choke up after the oil pump has been set on the liberal side (such as a new machine or rebore), and it is advisable to take this to pieces (three) and clean out thoroughly after 600 miles ; easiest method is to burn it out over an ordinary gasring or blowlamp.

In any case, clean regularly every 1,000 miles.

For increased efficiency and to minimise back pressure, you may increase the small $\frac{1}{4}$-inch hole at the end of the cone (inside portion) to about $\frac{3}{8}$ inch, and on the Flyers, which already have the expansion chamber at the front, the outer baffle of the inside part may be entirely removed, *but* this latter idea is not conducive to real silence, although careful driving (i.e. no hectic blinding in first or second gears !) will see you through.

Oil Pump Setting (Pilgrim)

Oil pump settings are usually a nightmare to the " new owner," and the " so many drops per minute " idea bewilders him more than ever, so we suggest the following as a more certain method.

On new (or rebored) engines, set the pump to give one drop of oil at every third pulsation at the " beak," i.e. one, two, then drop.

After running in, it can then be reduced to one drop at every fourth pulsation, i.e. one, two, three, then drop. (Or even less by that time, as obviously you will have got into the " swing " of things.)

The exhaust, of course, is a reliable guide—excessive blue smoke means too much, absence of smoke not enough.

A faint haze at low speeds (lift the half-compression lever momentarily and it should give an extra " puff ") is fairly safe, but just remember that if you are too generous in adding oil to your petrol, you may be smoking profusely, but not getting enough oil to the mains and big ends via the oil pipes ; so be very careful on this point.

A Useful Repair Hint

To replace worn engine chains, it is easier to attach new chain to old one and " follow on."   If no old one is available, remove top engin eplates, smear first dozen links of chain with stiff grease and thread over engine sprocket (this allows the chain to cling to the teeth instead of " piling up " at the back of crankcase).   In the case of 1931 Flyers and Supers, this greasing is not necessary, as a chain guide is now provided.

OTHER SCOTT FEATURES

The Scott Kick Starter, Twospeed and Threespeed Gearboxes, the Clutch, Chains and Cycle Parts will be dealt with in later articles.

BRAKES AND BRAKING

By A. F. Houlberg

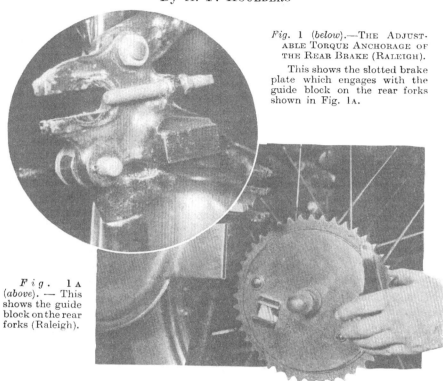

Fig. 1 (*below*).—The Adjustable Torque Anchorage of the Rear Brake (Raleigh).

This shows the slotted brake plate which engages with the guide block on the rear forks shown in Fig. 1A.

F i g. 1 A (*above*). — This shows the guide block on the rear forks (Raleigh).

IN the development of the motor-cycle almost every conceivable type of brake has at some time or other been employed. The searching tests imposed by the series of post-war T.T. races have gradually eliminated all designs of doubtful quality, so that the present-day motorcycle is almost invariably equipped with brakes which are perfectly sound in basic principle. The most casual of surveys of brake equipment at the last Motor Show will have revealed to the observer the almost universal use of the completely enclosed and well-protected internal expanding brake, clearly indicating that the days of such atrocities as wheel-rim brakes and belt-rim brakes are definitely a thing of the past. It is therefore not proposed to deal with such brakes at length in these pages, but

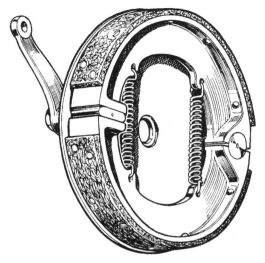

Fig. 2.—Typical Internal Expanding Motor-cycle Brake.

mainly to confine our attention to brakes of current design.

The internal expanding brake used on the modern motor-cycle consists of two shoes of semi-circular formation hinged together at one end and expanded into contact with the interior surface of the drum at the other, the method generally employed to expand the shoes being a rotating cam of substantially rectangular formation with well-rounded corners.

The First Points

A knowledge of the essentials of efficient braking mechanism will prove of great value to the owner in diagnosing the actual cause of any braking troubles he may encounter, and thus enable him to achieve a rectification in the shortest possible time. It is therefore considered that a few words on the fundamentals of brake design will not be amiss.

The Best Material for Brake Linings

In the first place, all brakes rely upon the existence of friction for their action, and it therefore follows that the quality of the friction, or, as it is technically known, the coefficient of friction, existing between the two elements of the

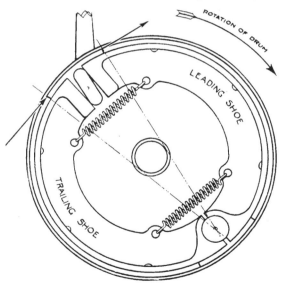

Fig. 3.—How Chatter Occurs.

This diagram clearly shows the forces acting on the two shoes due to rotation of the brake drum, and the reason why the leading shoe is applied with greater force than the trailing shoe, thus leading in certain cases to brake pick-up or chatter.

brake, namely, the stationary element and the rotating element, is of paramount importance. Many substances and combinations of substances have been employed from time to time, but the only material which can be said to give unqualified satisfaction in service is woven asbestos fabric. This asbestos fabric is often reinforced or bonded with brass wire, and highly compressed in the course of manufacture in order to increase its durability. The chief characteristics required of a friction material for brake purposes are that it should be able to resist high temperatures, that it should possess a high coefficient of friction, and that it should be hard wearing. The bonded asbestos brake lining possesses a happy combination of these three features. As a matter of interest, we give herewith a list of materials frequently used for frictional purposes, with their corresponding coefficients of friction :

Materials in Contact.	Coefficient of Friction.
Asbestos fabric on cast iron or steel	0·4
Leather on cast iron	0·2
Leather on aluminium	0·22
Cast iron on cast iron (lubricated)	0·1
Bronze on cast iron (dry)	0·21
Bronze on bronze (dry)	0·20
Hardwood on hardwood (dry)	0·48
Hardwood on hardwood (well lubricated)	0·16
Cast iron on hardwood (dry)	0·49
Cast iron on hardwood (slightly lubricated)	0·19
Cast iron on hardwood (well lubricated)	0·08

A Likely Cause of Sudden Brake Failure

From this table it will be seen, as is to be expected, that the question of lubrication between the frictional surfaces has a very important effect on the coefficient of friction, and thus upon the braking efficiency of the materials. For this reason, sudden ineffectiveness of a motor-cycle brake, if not due to an obvious external fault, can often be traced directly to a leakage of lubricant into the brake drum, due to over-zealousness with the oilcan or oilgun on the hubs or adjacent components. The remedies for this complaint will be discussed in detail later.

EXAMINING THE BRAKES

The Expanding Mechanism

If, upon examination, the lining is found to be in a good condition and free from foreign matter likely to impair its efficiency, attention should next be devoted to the expanding mechanism. As we have already indicated, this usually consists of a rectangular cam with rounded corners, which is centrally pivoted and operated through a short shaft by an external lever in connection with the operating mechanism. Irregularities in this cam, due to wear or neglect of lubrication, which would have the effect of stiffening its action, may frequently absorb so much of the energy applied to it that little is left for forcing the brake shoes themselves against the brake drum. The remedy for lack of lubricant is obvious, and consists, in cases which are not too severe, of the liberal application of an oilcan to the affected parts. In severe cases, dismantling the camshaft, thoroughly cleaning the bearings, greasing and reassembling are called for.

The Brake Cams

A not uncommon fault, which frequently is not immediately obvious (owing to the enclosed nature of most brake mechanisms), is occasioned by the cam working in an inefficient position. Normally, the cam should lie fairly snugly between the two parallel actuating faces forming the expanding ends of the brake shoes. This condition, however, is only attained with brake gear which has been particularly accurately made and with linings that are comparatively unworn. Immediately wear takes place, and the brake-actuating mechanism has been taken up accordingly, the cam assumes an angular position in relation to the ends of the brake shoes, and excessive wear or faulty manufacture may enable the cam to assume a position almost at right angles to the end faces of the shoes. Obviously, in this position the cam cannot impart additional movement to the shoes and, furthermore, it is in imminent danger of overshooting the safe " maximum " position and becoming locked in the " fully-on " position, so causing the brake to remain on, completely out of control of the rider. In all fairness to modern designers, it must be pointed out that the possibility of this occurring on present-day brakes is comparatively small. Nevertheless, faulty assembly of the brakes, or undue neglect,

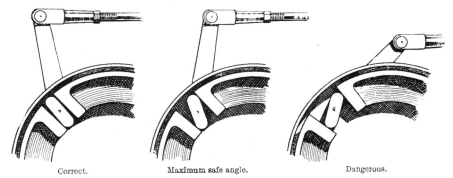

Correct.   Maximum safe angle.   Dangerous.

Fig. 4.—ATTENTION TO THE BRAKE OPERATING CAM.

The need for careful attention to the position of the brake operating cam relative to the two ends of the brake shoes is here clearly shown. It will be seen from the diagram on the extreme right that the cam is in imminent danger of turning right over.

Fig. 5.—Showing Rear Torque Arm.
The torque arm and its slotted anchorage to the frame on B.S.A. machines, also showing the spring-loaded fly-nut adjustment for the brake rod.

may yet produce this condition of affairs. The precise action of the cam, and the way in which it can become jammed after passing the dead-centre point, will be clearly followed on reference to the accompanying diagram.

How to check the Position of the Brake Shoes

As we have already indicated, there is some difficulty in observing the exact position of the shoes and expanding mechanism, owing to the fact that they are enclosed within the brake drum and brake back plate. The best way to ascertain the exact position of the expanding mechanism is to apply the brake moderately hard with everything assembled in the normal position and carefully mark on the back plate, or on a suitable piece of metal temporarily attached to it, the exact position of the lever. When the wheel is removed and dismantled, thus revealing the internal mechanism of the brake, it is an easy matter to move the lever into the position marked and to observe the relative position of the expanding cam and shoe ends. If an excessive gap is present between the shoe ends, causing the cam to assume a poor angle, this is generally due to wear of the brake-shoe lining (which should immediately be replaced), or may even be a combination of lining and brake-drum wear.

9

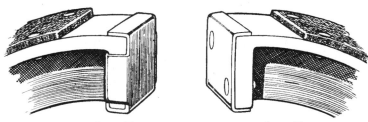

Fig. 6.—TWO METHODS OF PACKING THE SHOE ENDS.

That on the left consists of a cross-shaped piece of steel bent round the shoe end, and can be used when there is plenty of clearance on each side of the shoe. When this clearance is too small, the method depicted on the right may be employed. In this example, the packing is riveted to the shoe face with countersunk rivets finished flush.

When and how to pack the Ends of the Brake Shoes

In cases where examination reveals that the brake cam is nearly at the end of its effective travel and the brake lining shows little signs of wear, the brake may be restored to its original effectiveness by the use of packing at the shoe ends. Suitable packing pieces may easily be fashioned from mild steel sheet of correct thickness, taking care to see that they are fitted in such a manner that there is no likelihood of them leaving the shoe ends and thus upsetting the braking. The actual shape of these packing pieces will vary according to the design of the shoe, and it should not be outside the ingenuity of the average motor-cyclist to devise a suitable and firmly attached packing. Two methods of fashioning such packing pieces and attaching them to the shoe ends are indicated in the accompanying illustration, for your guidance.

Some manufacturers fit these packing devices as standard and provide accommodation for shims behind them, so that the cam position is adjustable, in which case it is only a matter of adding a correct number of shims of the right thickness to bring the brake back to its original efficiency.

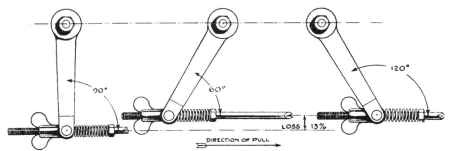

Fig. 7.—FAULTY POSITIONS OF BRAKE LEVERS.

These diagrams demonstrate the loss in effective leverage occasioned by faulty positioning of the brake operating levers relative to the brake pull rod. Losses of 10 per cent. are frequently encountered.

Brake Camshaft Lever Position—how it affects Braking Power

The factors controlling the effectiveness of any brake are the frictional area in contact with the brake-drum, the coefficient of friction between the shoe and the drum, the diameter of the drum and the pressure with which the shoe is forced against the drum. In the latter respect, too few riders appreciate the effect and importance of maintaining the correct angle between the brake camshaft lever and the pull rod or cable operating it. A close study of the diagram, showing the loss of effective leverage for different angles between the brake camshaft lever and the pull rod, will lead to an appreciation of the energy losses which can occur through neglect of this important point and the resulting loss of braking efficiency. It will be seen that the difference between a correct and incorrect angle may make as much as 13 per cent. difference to the force actually applied to the brake shoes, and thus to the braking efficiency.

It will be clearly seen from Fig. 7 that the most effective angle between the brake camshaft lever and its pull rod is 90°. Unfortunately, this is an ideal condition which is seldom constantly attainable in a brake, owing to the fact that a certain amount of motion must be permitted in order to apply the brake and a certain allowance must be made for wear. As usual, one has to compromise, and the most effective method is to allow the lever to lay backwards, making a relatively acute angle with the pull rod, so that when all clearances in the operating mechanism have been taken up and the brake shoes brought into contact with the drum, the lever and pull rod assume positions approaching the desired 90°. Care must, however, be exercised not to overdo the backward positioning of the camshaft levers, or so much power will be lost that it may become difficult to apply the brake. The limiting angles which the brake camshaft lever can make with the brake pull rod, to be reasonably effective, are clearly shown in the accompanying Fig. 7, from which it will be seen that it is unwise to allow the brake camshaft lever to make an angle of less than 60° or more than 120° with the pull rod. The maximum backward slope of the cam is always definitely controlled by the designer, and if the operating rod adjustment is slackened off until the brake camshaft is quite free, it will naturally assume this position under the action of the brake-shoe return springs. There is nothing to be gained by setting the lever beyond this point, as it will only expand the shoes slightly in the reverse direction and entail unnecessary lost motion during the brake application movement.

A FEW COMMON BRAKE FAULTS

Brake remaining constantly on

A brake which fails to come completely free from the brake drum when the brake is released is due to : (1) faulty adjustment or stiffness of the operating mechanism ; (2) excessive wear of the shoe pivots, allowing the

shoes to droop sufficiently for the heels of the lining to come in contact
with the drum; (3) the use of brake lining of the wrong thickness; (4)
badly fitted brake linings.

The remedy for the first is obvious, and merely entails the proper
manipulation of the brake adjustment and free use of an oilcan.

Wear of Shoe Pivots

Shoe pivot wear can be remedied by the employment of suitable
packing shims between the heel of the shoe and the anchorage pin, or,
better still, by fitting a new anchorage pin of larger diameter and a
reasonable fit in the heel of the shoe, so as to correctly reposition the shoe
in relation to the brake drum. When fitting anchorage pins of larger
diameter it must be remembered that the horns of the shoe ends may have
to be opened out to allow the
pin to find a seating in the
throat portion of the shoe end.

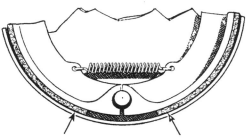

Fig. 8.—WEAR AT THE BRAKE SHOE ANCHORAGE.

When this becomes excessive, it may allow the
brake shoes to make constant contact with the
drum in the manner shown.

There is no remedy for the
use of too thick linings other
than their replacement. In
the course of time they will
naturally wear down to the
correct thickness, but, in the
meantime, ineffective brakes
will be the result, and the
heat generated by the points
of the shoes which remain in
constant contact with the
drum may be sufficient to
raise the temperature of the drum and the adjacent hub to such an
extent as to cause the hub grease to become sufficiently fluid to penetrate
the grease-retaining device and find its way on to the surface of the drums,
thus further reducing the braking efficiency.

Bad Fitting of Linings

This trouble is frequently encountered immediately after a brake has
been relined, due to carelessness on the part of the owner when riveting
up the linings on to the shoes. Faulty riveting of this nature often causes
local buckling of the lining, so that high spots are produced which remain
in constant contact with the brake drum. Such high spots can only be
remedied by removing the lining and carefully re-riveting.

High spots due to swelling of the lining round the rivet heads under
the action of riveting, are capable of satisfactory treatment if the swollen
lining is carefully hammered down on to the brake shoe while it is held
in a vice. Undue force should not be employed, particularly with the
modern aluminium brake shoe, or it will very likely be fractured.

Brake Fierceness or Chatter

A properly fitted and adjusted brake should be smooth and progressive in its action when it is applied with increasing force. Occasions arise, however, where brake action is unduly fierce and not under full control of the rider, producing a chattering action, which will cause a motor-cycle to come to an abrupt and erratic halt instead of pulling up smoothly. This type of faulty brake action is generally produced by what is very expressively termed " brake lining pick-up." What actually occurs is that the toe end of the leading shoe is picked up by the rotating brake-drum, which tends to carry it round with it until it encounters sufficient resistance from the brake-shoe pivot to cause it to release its grip. The released shoe now springs back to its normal position under the action of the take-off spring, only to be picked up again by the drum and repeat the action.

And the Remedy

Fig. 9.—When Oversize Anchorage Pins are Fitted.

Showing how the brake shoe ends should be treated. The metal should be removed from the horns of the shoe only and not from the throat. The metal should also be removed equally from either side.

Since the cause is the picking up of the shoe lining, the remedy rests with suitably treating the lining to obviate the possibility of the ends making such violent contact with the drum that the shoe will be carried round with such fierceness. The method employed to achieve this is to bevel off the ends of the linings, so that they make gradual contact with the drum when the brake is applied, for a distance of about 1 inch from the end, by means of a hack saw or rough file such as a " Dreadnought " milling file. If bevelling of the lining does not effect a cure, make sure that none of the rivets are proud of the lining and making contact with the drum. Also make sure that the take-off springs are not too weak, or that there is not undue slackness between the heels of the shoes and the pivot. In addition, the brake-shoe pivots should be examined to ascertain that they are not loose in the brake back plate.

Another Cause of Brake Chatter—Worn Brake Camshaft

Another source of chatter may originate from slackness in the operating mechanism when excessive wear has taken place between the brake camshaft and its bearing. Obviously, slackness at this point will enable a periodic motion of the shoes to take place under the action of the brake-drum.

Oil Leakage

An oil leakage into the brake drum may be the ultimate cause of a certain amount of brake chatter. When the oil becomes partly burnt off, it frequently reaches a critical stage, where violent brake chatter is produced.　The remedy in this instance is either to burn off the oil from the saturated lining with a blowlamp (care being taken not to melt the shoe if it is constructed of aluminium), or to soak the shoe and the lining in petrol until all the oil has worked out.

Dented Brake Drum

Brake chatter may again arise from defects in the brake drum itself. A brake drum which has become dented in a minor accident is always prone to picking up the leading shoe and producing chatter.　Here the obvious remedy is to get the brake drum trued up by skimming in a lathe if the damage is not too bad, or, if the brake drum is extensively damaged, to replace it by a new one, always remembering that it is inadvisable to take too much metal away from the brake drum, firstly, because such a procedure would weaken it unduly, and, secondly, it increases the clearance between the brake shoe and the brake drum, a condition of affairs which is liable to bring the expanding cam into an unfavourable position.

Brake Reaction—see that the Brake Back Plate is Firmly Anchored

The proper absorption of the brake reaction is a matter of no little importance.　It must be fully understood that the elementary laws of mechanics, as first laid down by Sir Isaac Newton, clearly define that every action has an equal and opposite reaction.　The retarding force, or braking action, applied to the wheel, produces an exactly equal and opposite reaction on the brake shoes which must be resisted by the brake-shoe anchorage pin and the brake back plate, to which it is usually anchored. In turn this back plate must be firmly attached to the frame to resist the reaction, and, furthermore, it should be so attached to the frame that undue bending moments—that is to say, forces tending to bend the frame out of truth—are avoided.　The majority of brakes have a torque rod, stud, or link, attached to the back plate, whose other end is anchored to a suitable point in the frame so as to absorb the torque reaction due to brake application, and in cases of persistent brake chatter, it is essential to make sure that the anchorage for the brake back plate is not loose but firmly tightened up.

One problem incidental to the design of the torque member arises from the necessity for chain adjustment in the case of the rear wheel, and the demand for simple wheel removal in the case of both wheels.　For this reason many manufacturers employ a form of torque anchorage consisting of a slotted member attached to the brake plate engaging a fixed pin attached to the frame, or a reversal of this scheme.　When the parts are new, and a good fit exists between the brake anchorage stop pin and the slot, so that little or no backlash exists between them, the production of chatter, due to looseness of the back plate, is unlikely.

In the case of machines that have seen some wear, however, there may be sufficient play between these parts to cause trouble of this nature, although it must be remembered that in all cases the tightening up of the spindle nuts will have a clamping effect on the back plate, and that provided these are kept done up dead-tight (an important point for many other reasons), little trouble is likely to be encountered from this source.

Faulty Hub Bearings may cause Erratic Braking

Another cause of erratic brake action of the chattering variety is occasioned by faulty adjustment of the hub bearings, permitting the brake drum to possess an unnecessarily excessive degree of movement in relation to the brake shoes. The remedy here is obviously careful adjustment of the hub bearings. While attending to bearings, it is as well, in the case of front-wheel brake chatter, to check

Fig. 10.—SLOTTED TYPE TORQUE ANCHORAGE ON FRONT BRAKE (NORTON).

The brake operating cable has been withdrawn for clearness. This incidentally demonstrates the convenience of the slotted type cable anchorage.

over the bearings of the steering head and make sure that excessive play has not developed in these.

Worn Shoe Pivot

Yet another cause of brake chatter is wear at the shoe pivot pin, permitting the two halves of the shoe to make contact with each other

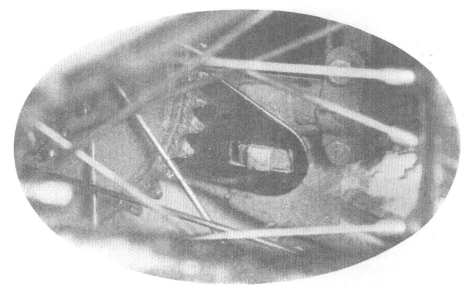

Fig. 11.—A.J.S. REAR BRAKE, SHOWING STUD AND SLOTTED ANCHORAGE.
Photo was taken from the right-hand side of machine through the rear wheel.

without making firm contact with the anchor pin, thus permitting the shoes to have a certain amount of play at the anchorage.

Excessive Brake Pedal or Brake Lever Movement

If an excessive movement of the brake pedal or brake lever is called for in order to bring the brakes into action, despite the fact that the clearance between the shoes and the drums has been accurately set, it indicates the existence of faulty adjustment or excessive wear in the operating mechanism. A certain amount of clearance or lost motion is of course necessary, but the discriminating rider will cut this down to the smallest possible amount, so that he has the brake under full control immediately he applies his foot to the pedal or hand to the lever, without the necessity for making an extensive movement in order to bring the brake into action. The modern motor-cycle brake has so few articulated joints in its make-up that the possibility of sufficient backlash or wear taking place in these appreciably to affect brake application is remote. In nearly every case it will be found that this fault is entirely due to incorrect adjustment on the part of the owner.

Straight Pull Rods should not require Frequent Adjustment

Brakes operated by pull rods which are practically inextensible should maintain their adjustment for a considerable time, since the only modification which takes place is that due to wear of the friction linings, and modern friction linings are capable of giving many thousands of miles' service before appreciable wear takes place.

A Note on Cranked Pull Rods

In a well-designed brake gear of the rod type, the pull rods will be arranged to be dead straight and to give as direct a pull as possible on the brake camshaft lever. There are, however, numerous examples in use where the brake rod is cranked in order to dodge a projecting portion of the motor-cycle's anatomy, in which case there is always present the tendency to straighten out the kinks. This will have the result of increasing the effective length of the pull rod, in which case fairly frequent attention to the brake adjustment is advisable.

Cable-operated Brakes

Cable-operated brakes, in spite of the increase in the size of the operating cables which has taken place in recent years, are still prone to a certain amount of stretch, particularly in the case where a rider drives on his brakes, instead of employing the more gentle and economical method of driving by correct manipulation of the throttle. Cable-operated brakes, therefore, need much more frequent attention in the matter of adjustment than rod-operated brakes.

Every maker provides ample and simple adjustment to meet all but exceptional eventualities, and the rider who permits his brake gear to reach the stage where an excessive amount of lost motion takes place before the brake comes into action, has only himself to blame.

General Adjustment

The simplest way to carry out braking adjustments is to put both front and rear wheels on the stand clear of the ground. Slacking the locking devices of the brake adjustment, it is then a fairly easy matter to tighten up the adjustments until the brakes are just heard rubbing, always taking care, of course, that the brake pedal or brake lever is hard up against its stop. It is then advisable to slack back the adjustments one complete turn to make sure that the brakes are completely clear of the drum when in the " off " position. A test of the brakes should then be carried out by depressing the brake or operating lever and turning the wheel by hand to obtain a rough idea of its effectiveness. The brakes should then be released and the wheel spun by hand to make certain that the shoes still clear the drum in the " off " position. If they do not, examine the brake mechanism for stiffness in the manner indicated elsewhere.

Rear-wheel Brake Adjustment

In the case of rear-wheel brakes the need for chain adjustment produces additional complications. The method of adjusting the chain

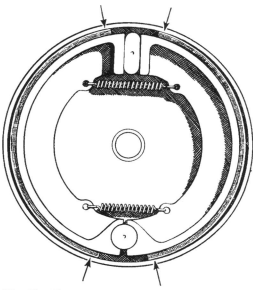

Fig. 12.—EFFECT OF RELINING WITH LINING TOO THICK.

Only the toes and heels of the lining are making contact with the drum, obviously a very inefficient state of affairs.

invariably consists in sliding the rear wheel backwards and forwards between the slotted fork ends, and it is not difficult to realise that this will make a complete readjustment of the brake necessary. Whenever chain adjustments are carried out, it is therefore essential to make a brake test and readjust the brake accordingly. When adjusting the chain it is also of importance to remember that if the torque member is of the rigidly clamped type, it should be firmly tightened up again after the chain adjustment has been completed. A certain amount of brake chatter may be produced if this point is neglected.

SPECIAL BRAKE ADJUSTMENTS

The Rudge-Whitworth Coupled Brakes

The Rudge - Whitworth concern have developed a form of coupled front and rear brakes which gives a high degree of braking efficiency if properly adjusted. The basis of this coupled brake scheme is the fact that the percentage of the total weight of the motor-cycle carried by the front wheel is increased on brake applica-

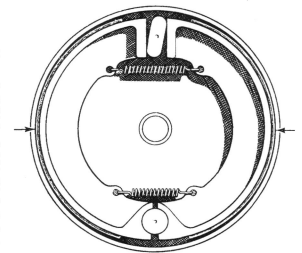

Fig. 13.—EFFECT OF EMPLOYING BRAKE LINING TOO THIN.

Here only the centres of the shoes make contact with the drum, so that ineffective brakes are the result.

tion, the extent of this additional load being of course dependent upon the violence of the brake application. In cases of very violent braking, the larger percentage of the total weight of the machine is thrown on to the front wheel, due to the momentum possessed by the cycle and rider, and it therefore becomes of some importance to have high braking power available on the front wheel. The Rudge device provides for equal brake application on both front and rear wheels under normal conditions, but ensures that a greater percentage of the braking effort is provided on the front wheel when the brakes are heavily applied. The scheme is extremely simple, and consists of a partly compressed spring interposed in the rear-brake pull rod, the strength of this spring being sufficient to overcome normal pressures applied to the brake pedal; in fact, the rear-brake pull rod functions as though it were solid, the spring remaining in the extended position. Under these conditions, pressure on the brake pedal applies both front and rear brakes equally. As increased pressure is applied to the pedal, however, the resistance of the coupling spring is overcome and it is further compressed. When this occurs little additional braking load is applied to the rear brake, but the majority of the additional braking effort is applied to the front wheel, thus enabling full use to be made of the increased load which the front wheel has now been called upon to bear.

This method of brake application has many commendable points, and certainly goes far towards providing maximum possible braking under all circumstances.

Adjusting Rudge-Whitworth Coupled Brakes

The brakes are adjusted in the normal way, the rear by means of a large hexagon adjusting nut on the brake camshaft lever, the differential action being automatically provided by the initial tension on the control spring which has been carefully selected by the manufacturers. The only point to note is that too much pressure must not be applied to the pedal while adjustment is taking place, if it is the habit of the owner to test the adjustment of the brakes by partly applying them and feeling the resistance offered by each wheel.

Another point to note is that the hand operation for the front brake must be attached to the anchorage on the brake camshaft lever nearest the camshaft, otherwise the hand operation will be excessively powerful and the balance of the foot operation affected.

The method recommended by the makers for adjusting these brakes is to place the machine on both front and rear stands, and ascertain that the pedal is tight up against its stop. The hexagon adjusting nuts on both front and rear brakes can then be adjusted up until the brakes begin to operate when the pedal is depressed approximately $\frac{1}{2}$ inch. Both brakes should come on together with equal force, but, if anything, the front brake should be given slight preference, that is to say, it should come

Fig. 14.—Showing Triangulation and Pivot Bolt on Norton Rear Wheel.

The well-designed torque rod arrangement on the Norton rear brake which relieves the frame of bending moments. Note the well-ribbed brake drum, ensuring freedom from distortion and good heat dissipation.

on slightly before the rear, as this leads to greater steadiness when braking on greasy roads. The hand control for the front brake may then be adjusted to correspond by means of its individual adjustment at the crown of the front forks.

" Matchless " Coupled Brakes

In the " Matchless " coupled braking system both the front-brake cable and rear-brake pull rod are attached to the brake pedal without any resilient connection. The adjustment advocated in this case is to arrange the brake adjustments so that the front brake is applied slightly before the rear, and the proportions of the brake levers are so adjusted that the braking effort applied to the front wheel is correct and always greater than that on the rear wheel. To obtain this adjustment both wheels should be jacked up and the knurled adjusting nuts screwed up with the brake pedal slightly depressed, until the braking is such that when it becomes difficult to rotate the front wheel, braking on the rear wheel is just becoming noticeable. If the adjustment has been correctly carried out both wheels will of course turn freely when the brake pedal is released. If they do not, it is an indication that the brake pedal was not depressed quite far enough while the adjustment was being carried out.   Should the tendency exist for the back wheel to skid upon fairly hard application of the brake, it is generally an indication that the adjustment of the front brake foot-operated cable is not sufficiently in advance of the rear, and the remedy in this event is either to tighten up the front foot-brake cable slightly or to slacken the rear-brake pull rod adjustment slightly.

Spring Frames and Braking

The introduction of a spring frame generally has the effect of complicating the braking system, since provision has to be made to ensure that the action of the frame has no modifying effect on the effective length of the brake pull rod mechanism.

Where cable operation is employed, little trouble is encountered in guarding against this difficulty, since all that is necessary is for the anchorage of the outer casing to be attached to some unsprung portion of the frame.

Where pull rod operation is employed, however, some device must be employed to overcome changes in the effective length of the pull rod occasioned by deflections in the sprung portion of the frame.   A case in point is to be found in the "Matchless" spring frame models, where a slotted link embraces an extension of the pivot pin on which the rear fork assembly hinges.   This ensures that the pull rod always passes through the centre of the pivot, and that the effective length of the rod remains the same.   A point to watch therefore in the case of brake adjustments with spring frames is the device employed for maintaining the pull rods in their correct positions, and to see that they are correctly located both before and after brake adjustment.

BRAKE REPAIRS

How to reline the Brake Shoes

The most frequent repair which the owner is called upon to carry out is relining the shoes with fresh friction lining.

Getting at the Shoes

Removal of the rear wheel will in some cases give access to the brake shoes.   In other cases it may be necessary to withdraw the brake back plate from the hub.   In nearly all front-wheel brakes withdrawal of the wheel and removal of the brake back plate is necessary.   The method of dismantling varies considerably with different makes, and this question is dealt with in detail elsewhere.

Examination of the brake shoes will in nearly every case reveal the fact that they are held in position against the cam and pivot pin by means of short coil springs in tension which are generally known as take-off springs.

Mark them before Removal

Before removing the shoes it is wise to mark them in such a manner that you will replace them in the same position. Shoes have a way of bedding down during use and, if they are reversed, may not work so sweetly as if retained in their original positions.

How to release Them

To release the shoes it is necessary to extend the springs until one shoe is pulled sufficiently far away from the cam and anchorage pin to clear any retaining disc, or discs, which maintain it in position, so that it may be moved sideways clear of the cam and pivot pin, thus releasing the other shoe. The retaining springs are never so strong that appreciable difficulty is likely to be encountered in separating the brake shoes in this way by hand, and it is a very much simpler method than trying to unhook the springs by means of a metal rod or a screwdriver.

In Cases of Special Difficulty

In cases where difficulty is encountered in withdrawing the brake shoes in this manner, recourse may have to be made to releasing the shoes by removing the springs, in which case a piece of stout string threaded through the eye of the spring will be found much the simplest method. Protecting the hand with a suitable quantity of rag padding, sufficient pull can be imparted to the string to extend the spring until the eye is clear of its anchorage on the brake shoe. When both springs are loosened in this manner the brake shoes are completely free.

Removing the Old Lining

The old lining can now easily be removed by gripping the brake shoe in a vice and inserting a cold chisel under one end, shearing the brake-lining rivets in sequence, taking care to hold the cold chisel at such an angle that the brake shoe will not be cut into, and remembering that it is necessary for the rivets to be sheared off close to the shoe or unnecessary difficulty may be experienced in withdrawing them. Once started the remainder of the lining is easily torn away from the rivets whose projecting portion can now easily be cut off with the cold chisel. With the lining removed and the rivets cropped off short, the remaining portion of the rivet can be punched through the flange of the brake shoe by means of a suitable rivet or nail punch.

The New Lining

Procure a sufficient quantity of lining of the correct width and thickness to reline the shoes, taking particular care that the thickness is correct. Too thick a lining may cause you to have difficulty in replacing the brake-drum in position at the end of the relining operation ; too thin a lining will prevent you from obtaining the maximum results from your brakes, since only the toes of the shoes will be coming into action. Replacement linings of the correct width and thickness, and frequently cut to length and moulded to the contour of the shoe, are obtainable from the manufacturers, and their use is advised whenever possible.

You will need some Rivets also

Procure also a sufficient quantity of copper or aluminium rivets with well-countersunk heads and with shanks of the right diameter. Proper brake-lining rivets are obtainable from most cycle stores of repute. Never attempt to use mild steel rivets for this work.

Cutting the Lining

The new lining should accurately be cut to length and bent to shape to fit snugly on to the shoe, when it can be correctly positioned and held in place at one end by means of toolmakers'

Fig. 15.—ARIEL, FRONT, SHOWING ANCHORAGE HALFWAY UP FORKS.

The torque link is anchored well up the fork blade, and is disposed at an angle which throws the minimum bending loads on the blades. This illustration also clearly indicates the combined rod and Bowden cable operation employed to avoid the possibility of mud clogging the cable portion of the operating mechanism.

clamps or similar devices. To facilitate bending the lining, it is advisable to warm it slightly. A drill is now brought into use of the same diameter as the rivet shank, and using the rivet holes in the brake shoe flange as a guide, holes to accommodate the two end rivets are drilled in the lining, taking care to see that the lining is laying parallel to the edge of the shoe.

Countersink the Holes in the Lining

Since it is imperative that the heads of the rivets should remain clear of the brake drum to avoid scoring the surface of the drums and reducing the braking efficiency, it is necessary to countersink the holes just made

Fig. 16.—How to treat the Ends of the Linings to obviate Pick-up or Chatter.

The linings should be bevelled off in the manner here shown.

in the linings to receive the countersunk heads of the rivets. Two methods may be employed to effect this. A large drill or rose-type countersink may be employed to countersink the mouths of the holes, but by far the best way is to use a large centre punch and to produce a countersink by hammering it into the hole just made. This method of countersinking does not damage the ends of the fibres forming the brake lining to the same extent as the other method ; in fact, it tucks the loose ends inwards, where they become firmly gripped by the conical head of the rivet.

Riveting the Lining in Place

Inserting the rivets into the holes just countersunk, they may be riveted over on the inside of the brake flange. This is best accomplished by holding in the jaws of a vice a short length of rod of a diameter equal to the diameter of the head of the rivet, and using this as an anvil upon which to rest the rivet head while the shank is being hammered over. This will ensure that the head of the rivet will bed firmly on its countersunk seating in the lining, and, furthermore, that its head is well below the working surface of the lining. Having riveted up the first two rivets to your satisfaction, you may remove the clamps, and place them farther round the shoe, taking care that the lining is kept in firm contact with the shoe flange the whole time. You may then drill and countersink the next hole, insert the next rivet, and continue in this way until you have completed the whole of the riveting.

Three Points to Watch

Three points must be closely watched during the riveting process. The first is that the lining beds firmly on the shoe flange for the whole of its length and is devoid of buckles ; the second is that no rivets should remain proud of the lining, and the third is that no local swelling of the lining has taken place round the rivet holes during the riveting process. Any high spots of the nature produced by the latter process would prevent the brake from being wholly effective and, to guard against this, it is necessary to smooth off all such local swellings with the help of a file before replacing the brake shoes.

Giving a Workmanlike Finish

To avoid harshness of brake action, it is also advisable to bevel off the ends of the linings slightly before replacing the shoes. This is best accomplished by gripping the relined shoe in the jaws of a vice, and taking down or bevelling the ends with the help of a hacksaw used with its blade lying almost flat on the surface of the lining.

STIFFNESS OF BRAKE APPLICATION—CAUSES AND CURES

Bad Lubrication

The more general cause of this complaint is lack of lubricant at the essential bearings of the brake gear, and the first step therefore is the liberal application of oil or grease to all joints of the braking mechanism.

Other Causes

If this treatment fails to effect a cure, the next step is to disconnect the operating mechanism from the brake camshaft lever. It is then a simple matter to find out where the stiffness exists in the operating mechanism by operating the brake lever or pedal by hand, when any stiffness in this section of the brake can readily be felt. In the case of rod-operated mechanisms, stiffness is probably due to tightness between the pedal and its bearing, or between the forks and eyes of the pull rod. Stiffness may also be occasioned by minor accidents, which have been the cause of bending the brake pedal shaft or the brake pull rod, and it will not be found difficult to trace either of these latter complaints. Complete dismantling of the brake gear, cleaning and greasing of the bearings, and rectification of any irregularity in alignment is the remedy called for.

Stiffness in Cable-operated Brakes

In the case of cable-operated brakes, stiffness is generally due to lack of lubricant between the stranded cable and its casing. This condition is clearly indicated when the brake lever fails to return to the " off " position smartly, when it is released after application. The obvious remedy is the introduction of suitable lubricant between the cable and casing. The best way to accomplish this is to withdraw the cable from the lever, usually not a difficult matter, procure a funnel with a spout large enough to slip comfortably over the nipple and the outer cable, then procure a cork of the right diameter to fit into the end of the funnel spout, and bore through its centre a hole of the

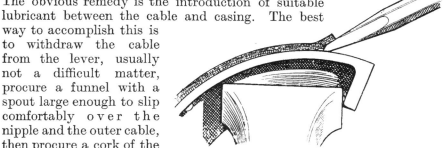

Fig. 17.—Removing an Old Brake Lining and Shearing the Retaining Rivets.

Care must be taken to see that the bevelled cutting edge of the cold chisel lies flat on the face of the shoe to avoid damaging the surface of the shoe.

10

same diameter as the outside diameter of the outer casing. If the cork is slipped over one end of the outer casing (it may be necessary to split the cork down one side to do this), and the funnel forced on to it in the manner shown in our illustration, a quantity of oil may be poured into the funnel, which will finally permeate the space between the cable and the outer casing if the assembly is allowed to remain in the vertical position for some time. Complete saturation of the cable will be indicated as soon as oil begins to trickle out from the lower end.

A Tip for Easy Lubrication

There are on the market fitments which can be introduced permanently

Fig. 18.—ENFIELD, REAR BRAKE, SHOWING SLOTTED LINK ARRANGEMENT.
Here the frame member is slotted and the brake torque arm is rigidly bolted to it.

into the outer casing, whereby the introduction of lubricant by grease gun is rendered possible as a matter of routine. The owner who takes a pride in the sweetness of operation of his machine will find it worth while to incorporate these small and inexpensive fitments in his cable layout.

More about Cable-operated Brakes

Most cable mechanisms for brake operation have a telescopic member enclosing a coil return spring introduced in their length. Examination of this fitment should be made for complete freedom. These telescopic members are often in a very exposed position, where they become encased with mud and road dirt to such an extent as to interfere with their free action. If one end of the cable is released from its anchorage—and this can generally be done without removing the nipple by pulling on the wire until the nipple is clear, and slipping the cable through the slotted portion of the anchorage—sufficient freedom is given to the outer cable to enable the two halves of the telescopic member to be withdrawn from each other for cleaning purposes. After cleaning, a liberal application of grease is of course advantageous.

Before Reassembling test the Brake Camshaft Mechanism

Before reconnecting the brake-operating mechanism to the brake camshaft levers, test the brake camshaft and shoe assembly for freedom of action. This is readily accomplished by applying pressure on the camshaft lever with the hand, and noting whether it returns smartly to the " off " position when released. Any sluggishness here indicates either that the brake camshaft bearing is binding, due to dirt, lack of lubricant, or distortion, or that dirt has found its way into the interior of the brake drum, where it is interfering with the freedom of action of the brake shoes.

When both the operating mechanism and the brake shoe mechanism return snappily to the " off " position after application, you may reconnect the brake, which should then provide satisfactory working.

The Causes of Ineffective Brake Action

Brakes whose effectiveness of action are below normal owe their lack of braking ability to either of the following causes :

(1) Oil or grease which has found its way on to the linings by overzealousness on the part of the owner with the oilcan or grease gun, or faulty oil-retaining devices.

(2) Linings which have worn to such an extent that the brake shoes can no longer be expanded into contact with the brake drum effectively.

(3) Operating levers at inefficient angles (this is generally caused by the previous fault, namely, worn linings).

(4) Damaged brake-drums.

(5) Bad riveting, which has permitted the lining rivets to become proud of the lining and thus make contact with the brake-drum, preventing the friction lining from carrying out its proper function.

Remedies

Linings which have become saturated with oil can be rendered serviceable again in the manner detailed on page 138.

The remedy for worn linings is obviously their replacement, and this has already been dealt with in detail in these pages.

Levers at the wrong angle are usually caused by worn linings, and their remedy is therefore relining, as in the previous case.

Damaged brake drums are generally more difficult to detect and rectify. High spots on the drums, such as those caused by a dent produced by a blow, can usually be seen when the wheel and drum are

the solder is just melted, and pulling the nipple off the wire with a pair of pliers. Since, for the purposes of safety, the ends of the wire strands are almost invariably hammered over, it is well to remember that it is easier to remove the nipple towards the end where the breakage has taken place.

Examine the Nipples

When the nipple is removed carefully examine its interior by holding it up to the light and make sure that it is well tinned, and that the solder has covered the whole of its interior. If the interior is in any way defective, employ a new nipple.

Fig. 21.—RALEIGH, FRONT, SHOWING CLAMPED TORQUE ARM.

Also shown is the ingenious adjustment for the cable, consisting of a shouldered bolt working in a guide.

First solder One Nipple on to End of New Cable

Having obtained a suitable quantity of the right-size cable, you may solder one of the nipples on to one end of the new wire. This is not generally a difficult matter, since the ends of the wire, when bought, are invariably already well tinned, that is to say, covered with solder. All that is necessary is to slip the nipple on to the end of the wire, so that approximately $\frac{1}{8}$-inch of cable projects from the nipple head; apply a suitable quantity of flux—a non-corrosive flux, such as Fluxite, being recommended—and with a soldering iron of not too small dimensions, sufficient heat and solder can be applied to the nipple to make a sound joint. Make sure that the solder is running well through the nipple, so that the maximum length of joint is made with the wire. You may now open out and hammer down the short strands of the cable protruding from the head of the nipple, finally embedding them in a blob of solder introduced with the iron, thus imparting to the head of the nipple a nice clean domed appearance, and effectively preventing the cable from being drawn through the nipple.

Next thread the New Cable into Position

The next step is to thread the cable through the attachment to the brake camshaft lever (usually a forked fitting), through the return spring (when one is provided), through the cable adjuster (after this latter item has been screwed right down so that the maximum adjustment is provided), and through the cable outer casing. It is then an easy matter to pass it through the keyhole-type slot, with which practically all brake-operating levers are provided.

Now measure off the Exact Length Required

An accurate measurement of the length of the cable required can now be made, and the next step is to cut the cable to length.

Tin the Cable near the Proposed Cut

In preparing the cable the strands are imparted a certain amount of tension, which causes the cable to unravel itself immediately it is cut. To avoid this, the cable should be well tinned for a distance of at least 2 inches on either side of the proposed cut, so that the strands are firmly embedded in solder and thus prevented from spreading. The cable naturally has to be withdrawn from the hand lever for this purpose.

How to cut the Cable

The highly tempered wire from which brake cables are made is some-what difficult to cut ; only the best wire-cutting pliers on the market are able to deal with these with certainty. The best medium to employ to cut this wire is a cold chisel used in conjunction with a suitable steel cutting block. To prevent undue fraying of the ends of the cable during cutting, which could interfere with the passing of the remaining nipple over the end into its correct position, the use of a cutting block provided with two grooves at right angles across its face which intersect near the middle of the block is advocated. These grooves should be of a width closely approximating the diameter of the cable to be cut, so that it is restrained on either side during the cutting process close up to the cut. The method of employing this block is to lay the tinned cable in one groove, with the point where it is desired to effect the cut lying in the centre of the other groove. The cold chisel is then rested upon the cable in the centre of the cross groove and given a smart blow with the hammer. This should sever the cable quite cleanly if the chisel is sharp and the tinning has been well carried out.

Fig. 22.—Fitting a Cable Nipple.

Before cutting the cable, solder it for about 2 inches on each side of the proposed cut. This will prevent the strands unravelling. Then cut the cable, slip nipple into position and spread the ends of the cable as shown above.

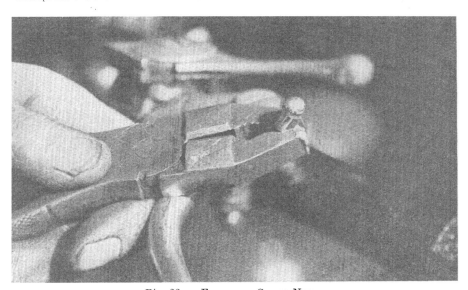

Fig. 22a.—Fitting a Cable Nipple.

Next apply solder to the cleaned ends of the cable and nipple. The solder should form a neat ball as shown.

Fig. 23.—THE MATCHLESS COUPLED BRAKE.

Clearly showing the double-armed pedal and the connection of the front-brake cam and rear-brake pull rod thereto. The illustration also clearly shows the slotted link embracing the spring frame pivot, which ensures that the effective length of the rear-brake pull rod remains constant.

Rethread the Cable into Position

The cable should be now threaded through any members from which it was removed for the cutting process, with the exception of the keyhole-type slot which forms a final anchorage to the brake lever.

The Second Nipple

The nipple should now be threaded on to the end of the cable, leaving $\frac{1}{8}$ inch projecting, as before, and treated in exactly the same way as the first end.

The Final Adjustment

When you have satisfied yourself that a sound joint has been made between the nipple and wire cable, you may, by pulling on the nipple with a pair of pliers, extend it sufficiently to pass beyond the end of the keyhole slot so that the cable can be passed through the throat of the slot, thus permitting the nipple to engage in its socket under the pull of the cable. If the nipples are lightly hammered home in their sockets before final adjustment of the brake takes place, it will ensure that the owner is not inconvenienced on the road due to the nipples slipping farther into their sockets on the first heavy brake application, thus upsetting the adjustment.

Band Brakes

These employ woven asbestos friction linings of a similar type to that used for internal expanding brakes, and the method of fitting it to the band is exactly the same.

ENGINE NOISES, AND WHAT THEY TELL

By W. C. Haycraft

Fig. 1.—Two Causes of Piston Slap.

The two pistons are examples of how wear takes place, and where this may be looked for. The one held in the hands shows the amount of wear that has taken place in the top ring groove. It is also an excellent example showing the result of piston "slap." Note how the metal has worn away above the top ring owing to the piston crown striking the cylinder wall. The other piston shows an extreme case of piston ring groove wear.

WITH an engine in proper order the only sounds which should be emitted when running are the slight hiss at the air intake, the click of the valves closing, and the subdued boom from the exhaust. Noises other than these are usually indicative of some trouble, and the exact nature of the trouble can often be determined by listening carefully to the noise emitted. In doubtful cases a sound stick is sometimes employed, but most motor-cycle engine faults can be located without this.

Piston " Slap "

With some engines having aluminium pistons there is present, in addition to the above-mentioned noises, a certain noise resembling the tapping of a pencil on a teacup. This noise, which is generally called piston "slap," if it disappears once the engine has reached its normal working temperature, can be disregarded. If it persists, it must be regarded as definite evidence of a worn piston or a worn cylinder, so allowing the piston to rock slightly (Fig. 1) during its stroke.   There should be no piston " slap " with cast-iron pistons.

Exhaust Note

The quality of the exhaust note often provides a useful index as to the general condition of the engine.   It should be crisp and clear.   If it sounds " woolly," it is likely that there are considerable carbon deposits present, or perhaps the exhaust valve is not seating properly.   If, on the other hand, the exhaust has a very low note, the pipe gets very hot (sometimes redhot), with occasional flames visible, and the engine gives an impression that it *could* but will not deliver full power, i is practically certain that the ignition is excessively retarded and the timing should be checked.

Banging in Exhaust

This noise (often erroneously referred to as " back-firing ") is, except when there is also misfiring, proof of either the escape of some of the mixture undergoing compression due to the exhaust valve not seating perfectly, or of incomplete combustion and overrichness of the mixture and its subsequent expulsion into and ignition in the exhaust pipe. There would probably also be a considerable amount of black or brown smoke issuing from the exhaust, sure proof of an overrich mixture. Such smoke contains much of the deadly carbon-monoxide gas.   Misfiring, due to a faulty sparking plug or a magneto defect, will also produce explosions in the exhaust system.

Banging in the exhaust can also be due to exceedingly late ignition timing, and if by mischance the ignition has been timed on the exhaust instead of on the compression stroke, a series of violent exhaust bangs may be the only signs of life exhibited by the engine.

Popping Back at Carburetter

This peculiar noise, which is sometimes accompanied by a small blue flame issuing from the air intake, may be due to several causes. If the hand be held close to the intake it is usually found that it becomes quite moist with petrol vapour thrown back from the induction pipe. The most common cause of popping or spitting back is a weak mixture, but it may also be due to a sticking inlet valve, or in some cases a weak inlet valve spring.   Loss of power would, of course, be present in any case, and when the valve or spring is at fault some loss of compression would be apparent with perhaps misfiring.   A slight squeak also usually accompanies a sticking inlet valve.

Knocking

EARLY IGNITION.—Several kinds of engine knocks occur besides piston " slap," and they may be due to a variety of causes, chief among which are : pre-ignition, caused by carbon deposits ; an unsuitable sparking plug ; defective combustion ; excessive lubrication ; too early an ignition timing ; incorrect valve clearances ; too high a compression ratio ; or the temporary incandescence of metallic irregularities. Pre-ignition knock is easily recognisable, the sound resembling the tapping of a light hammer on an anvil. Pre-ignition usually occurs when hill climbing, or when the engine is driven rather slowly under load. Pre-ignition is definitely harmful, and must not be allowed to continue for any length of time or damage will follow.

WORN BEARINGS.—Another kind of engine knock sometimes mistaken for pre-ignition is the knock due to worn bearings.   In this case, however, the somewhat different noise produced and the impossibility of eliminating it by ordinary methods makes it fairly simple to detect.

Mechanical knocks of this kind may be due to slack connecting rod or crankshaft bearings.

BIG-END BEARING.—If the big-end bearing of the connecting rod is at fault, it will be found that the noise, though similar to that caused by pre-ignition, is slightly more dull, and occurs once every two engine revolutions.   Moreover, if the throttle be suddenly closed, the knocking may not at once cease, and there may be some vibration felt.

SMALL-END BEARING.—If the small-end bearing is at fault, a slight rattle of the gudgeon pin may be audible when the engine is quickly decelerated.

HISSING NOISES.—Any hissing noise, apart from that at the air intake when depressing the kick-starter, is an indication of gas leakage past the valves or piston rings.

Thumping and Whining Noises

Slack crankshaft bearings are indicated by a thumping noise similar to that produced by a heavy substance hitting the ground, and the noise usually occurs once every engine revolution.   If a crankshaft bearing becomes loose in its housing, this may be indicated by an intermittent or continual screeching noise, and the metal in the vicinity of the bearing may become very hot.   The noise produced by crankshaft end float, which is not of great importance unless excessive, is a muffled and irregular knock.

A noise very similar to piston " slap " is that occasionally caused by slight up-and-down movement of worn piston rings in their grooves.   A high-pitch singing or whirring noise, accentuated with increase of engine speed, usually denotes a worn timing gear.

The tap made by valve mechanism is easily recognised, for the noise obviously has an exterior origin, and coincides with the opening or closing of a valve.   It may denote worn cams or tappets, excessive valve clearances, worn rockers, worn valve stems, broken springs, and so on.

REPAIRING AND OVERHAULING J.A.P. ENGINES

By STANLEY GREENING, A.M.I.A.E. (*J. A. Prestwich Ltd.*)

NOTES ON DECARBONISING

Removing S.V. Cylinder

REMOVE exhaust-pipe nuts and valve caps. Disconnect petrol pipes and take off carburetter from induction pipe. On twin engines the induction pipe is fitted with two taper collars, the nuts being bored with a corresponding taper. These must be removed, both being right-hand threads.

Valve Caps

It is advantageous to remove the valve caps while the cylinder is fixed on the crankcase, as there is then less likelihood of damaging the base. Should the exhaust-pipe nuts and valve caps be difficult to remove, run the engine a little to warm it up, then work a little paraffin down the threads. If the valve caps are of aluminium it is better to let the engine cool down again before removing them, as the contraction and expansion of aluminium is much greater than that of cast iron.

Take off cylinder fixing nuts, removing them diagonally across the base in order to prevent throwing undue strain on one side.

Taking off Cylinder

The cylinder can now be taken off, but care must be exercised when doing this to see that no strain is thrown on the connecting rod. It is easier if the piston is practically on bottom dead centre of the stroke with machine in gear, not forcing the cylinder in any way, but gently levering it to the best position so that it will lift off easily.

Decarbonising

Now place a rag under piston and pack it round tightly so that no dirt or carbon can get into the crankcase. The piston top can then be scraped clean, but see that the crown is not scratched badly when doing this operation. Do not remove the rings unless you suspect

Fig. 1.—A USEFUL TOOL FOR REMOVING VALVE SPRINGS ON J.A.P. ENGINES.

that they require renewing, as they will be nicely bedded in, and there is a danger of distorting them if the operation is not performed very carefully.

Fig. 2.—A Useful Tip for handling a J.A.P. Engine when it is removed from the Frame.

A wooden block bolted to the bench by the side of the vice, as shown above, will enable the engine to be conveniently supported.

Removing Valves

The valves can be removed from cylinders; the best method, if a special tool is not available, is to place the cylinder upside down on the bench, placing a packing piece under the valve heads so that when compressing the spring the valve will be prevented from being forced out.

If a slot is cut in a piece of tube as shown in Fig. 1, this can be placed over the stem of the valve, then the spring compressed and cotter removed, leaving the spring and collar free, when valve can be taken out.

Grinding in Valves

The valve heads and cylinder can now be scraped free of all carbon and the valve seatings reground by placing a little valve grinding paste on the seats, rotating the valve with a screwdriver, and during the operation turning the valve in a clockwise and anticlockwise direction and periodically lifting the valve in order to prevent scoring

Fig. 3.—Removing the Bevel Drive.

In the case of engines fitted with the bevel-drive magneto, the drive is dismantled as follows : first remove the three bevel cap-cover screws, next shift the magneto to the left, now remove the bevel fixing nut, using a box spanner. Finally, use a brass punch, as shown above, to loosen the bevel wheel from its spindle.

the seats.   Do not place too much pressure on screwdriver, but turn sharply backwards and forwards.

Reassembling

The valves can now be reassembled in the cylinder after cleaning everything very thoroughly. It must be borne in mind that absolute cleanliness is essential in anything appertaining to engine work, and too much stress cannot be laid upon this point. Should the valve grinding compound get into the cylinder bore it will harm the latter and probably be washed into the bearings and quickly wear them out.

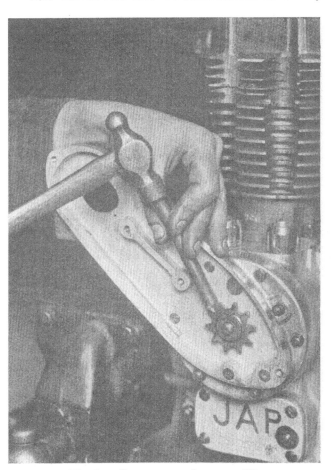

Fig. 3A.—Remove the Sprocket Wheel.

First remove the chain cover, next remove the sprocket nut, then use a brass punch and hammer to loosen the sprocket, as shown above.

The springs, cotters and collars can be replaced with the special tool, and cylinder refitted. Care must be taken to see that the piston does not foul the connecting rod. The ring gaps should be evenly spaced and the gap held closed on the piston while cylinder is gently pushed down over them. There is a big chamber on the mouth of J.A.P. cylinder bores which facilitates this operation.

No paper washers are used on any J.A.P. engines, but if the faces are

damaged the burrs can be eased off with a
fine Swiss file and a little goldsize smeared
on cylinder base.

When replacing the fixing nuts tighten
them finally a little at a time at opposite
corners.

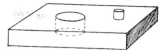

Fig. 4.—This illustrates a
Cast-iron Block used in dismantling the Flywheels
(see page 168).

COMPLETE OVERHAUL OF SINGLE AND TWIN S.V. ENGINES

Taking off Cylinders for a Complete Overhaul

After taking out the engine from the frame it can be conveniently held
in a vice if a wooden block is fixed to the bench as shown in Fig. 2.

Grip the middle left-hand lug in the vice with the gear side facing
forwards, keeping the bolt fixed in the opposite lug and resting the bottom
lug on the right-hand side of engine on the wood block. Cylinders
can now be dismantled, taking precautions to see that the pistons are
not forced against connecting rod in so doing.

Piston Rings

Remove the rings by inserting three feeler pieces between the rings
and piston, spacing them at equal distances and sliding the rings
over them. There is a very good instrument called the " Brico," manufactured by the British Chuck and Piston Ring Co., for this purpose.

Lay the rings aside so that they are fitted in their original grooves.

Taking off Sprocket

Next remove the chain-cover fixing screws and take off cover. The
sprocket on the half time shaft can now be dismantled by a sprocket
drawer or may be tapped at the *bottom* of the teeth with a brass punch
and a hammer. A sharp blow will remove this from
the taper after the fixing nut has been taken off. It
will be unnecessary to take off the magneto sprocket
unless the magneto requires attention.

How to take down the Bevel Drive

Various engines are fitted with a bevel drive
magneto. It is first necessary in this case to remove
the three bevel cap-cover screws, when the bevel fixing
nut on the cam-wheel spindle will be in view. This
must be removed with a box spanner, after having
taken off the magneto from its base so that the nut is
easier to get at. A sharp tap with a brass punch on
the bottom of the teeth in an anticlockwise direction
will remove the bevel from the taper.

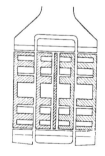

Fig. 5.—Big-end
Assembly.

Note position of
roller cages.

11

Fig. 6.—Remember this when removing the Timing Cover.

Before removing the timing cover the exhaust valve lifter must be raised as shown.

Exhaust Lifter and Chain Drive or Timing Cover

Now take off the nipple, nut and guide from the exhaust lifter spindle. Remove the nuts from the gear drive and gently tap off the drive. Do not place a lever between the drive and crankcase, as damage will most likely result. While tapping off the drive make sure that the exhaust lifter cam is free, by pulling the spindle up and finding the free position (see Fig. 6). Take out cam wheel and levers, and place the levers on one side in their correct positions. They can be refitted incorrectly, and it saves time to have them in correct order (see Fig. 8).

Removing Pinion

Place two dead-flat pieces of material on top of crankcase (see Fig. 16), and bring the piston

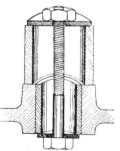

Fig. 7.—A Useful Workshop Tool for withdrawing or inserting Plain Bushes.

down on to these. The piston must be brought to rest by turning the engine in the direction in which it runs, and the nut can be removed from the pinion, remembering that this has a LEFT-HAND thread.

Remove the pinion from the taper, noting the keyway which is connected with the key on the gear spindle, as there are three keyways on the pinion, each one giving a variation in the valve timing. The very early type pinions were screwed on the shaft with a *left-hand* thread and had no fixing nut.

Fig. 8.—INSPECTING THE CAM GEAR.

After examining the teeth for backlash, remove the pinions and examine the levers for wear on the pads and on the cam-lever spindles. This picture also shows the order in which the levers should be replaced on their spindles when reassembling.

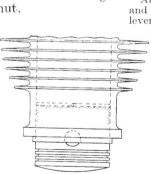

Fig. 9.—CHECKING PISTON-RING GAP.

Removal of Gudgeon Pin and Piston

In all standard engines prior to 1925 the gudgeon pins were a driving fit; aluminium pistons up to year 1928 were a fully floating fit with end pads in the gudgeon pins. After this date all J.A.P. pistons are fitted with circlips, which can be removed by compressing the two tail pieces and working outwards. Remove pin and take off

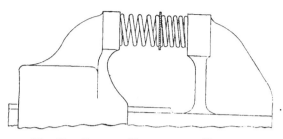

Fig. 10.—Testing Valve-spring Tension.

piston, marking the side which is facing the front and replacing in the same position.

Parting Crankcase

Now take all the fixing bolts from the crankcase, and the halves can be parted by gently tapping the projecting lug evenly with a lead hammer or mallet.

Main Bearings

Practically all types of J.A.P. engines are of the roller-bearing type on the main driving-shaft side, and plain phosphor bronze bush on the gear side.

On 8-h.p. side-valve twin engines the driving side was of the double-row ball-bearing type since the year 1920, and roller bearing on the smaller twin engines, such as 680 c.c. and 750 c.c.

The driving side must be gently tapped off the shaft if of the ball-bearing type, but can be easily lifted off the roller type.

Flywheels

The flywheels can now be taken apart for examination of big end. A cast-iron block is used as shown in Fig. 4, with a hole for the main-

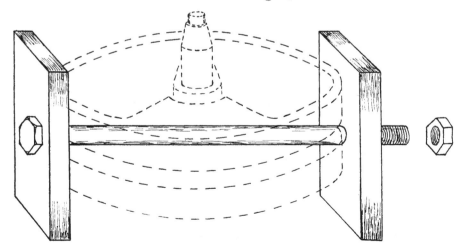

Fig. 11.—Truing Flywheels.

This useful workshop tool ensures that both flywheels are flush with one another.

Fig. 12.—Driving in the Liner of a Big End.

Note the distance piece placed between the jaws to prevent damaging the big end, and the mild steel bar interposed between the hammer and the liner to avoid damaging it.

shaft and a projecting peg which rests against the counter weight and prevents the flywheels from turning when taking off the crankpin nut. The block should be held in a vice with the peg uppermost.

After the nut is taken off, tap the flywheel a few times on the rim on opposite sides of the crankpin. This will loosen the flywheel and allow it to be withdrawn from the crankpin.

Big-end Bearings

The single-cylinder side-valve engines have a double row of rollers in separate cages, the twins have one in each side of the fork rod and two on the centre rod.

Inspection for Wear

All the parts should be inspected for wear and renewed as found necessary. No hard-and-fast rule can be applied to the parts that should be replaced. It must rest entirely upon whether the owner requires the engine to be made as new or if he requires as little as possible expended on replacements. However, where the mainshaft and big end are concerned, it is false economy not to renew the parts showing any wear at all, as it will necessitate the whole engine again being stripped for renewals. Should only one roller be scored or flaked, it will be policy to replace all of them, as only under microscopical inspection can it be proved if the others are affected, and as a rule they are, and the race also. The liners are pressed into the rod and can be tapped out, not forgetting to support

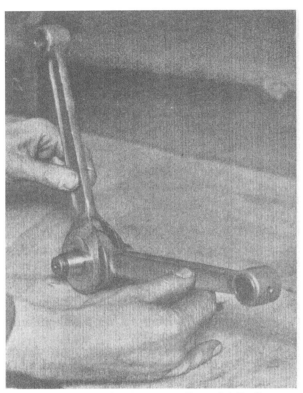

Fig. 13.—Con-rod Assembly for Twin J.A.P. Engine.
Note the extended slot which must be on the *inner* side
of the forked rod.

each half of the fork rod. Look to small end for wear in the bush. If requiring renewal, these and all plain bushes can be removed by the bolt and distance piece (see Fig. 7), or a suitable punch with pilot a good fit in the bush.

Cam Gear

Inspect cam gear: (1) teeth for back lash (oversize pinions can be had from makers); (2) levers for wear on the pads, or in case of roller cam levers on the outside diameter of rollers and on roller spindle. There should be appreciable up-and-down movement of the cam rollers on their bearings to allow for lubrication; (3) wear on cam-lever spindles and in bore of cam lever (a slight up-and-down movement is permissible here); (4) the exhaust lifter cam should show little sign of wear; (5) wear of cam-wheel spindle and bushes. It is best to place the cam wheels in the bushes, and after placing on the drive, test by trying to move the spindle up and down.

Cylinders and Pistons

Taking now the cylinders and pistons. Should the bore be badly stepped where the rings travel, it is advisable to have the cylinders reground and new pistons and rings fitted by the makers. This, however, should not be apparent until after several thousand miles running.

On 70 m/m bore and under the bottom of skirt clearance is approximately ·004 to ·006 inch. Above this diameter it is from ·007 to ·009 inch.

Rings can be tried for width of gap by placing the rings in the bore where it is not unduly worn and squaring them by placing the piston in the bore and pushing the rings down a little (see Fig. 9). These should be renewed if the gap exceeds $\frac{1}{32}$ inch. A fair average gap for all standard types of engines is ·005 per inch of bore diameter.

Piston-ring grooves should be tried by placing the ring in the groove and noting the amount of side play. When new this is ·002 to ·003 inch. It should not be excessive, as once it gets bad the groove very quickly wears by the change

Fig. 14.—How J.A.P. Pistons are tested for Wear.

The above gauge is used for measuring the diameter of a piston accurately at different points round the circumference. The large disk seen above the piston is hollow, and is closed by a flexible diaphragm which has a pointer touching the piston. The disk is connected to a thin tube, and both are filled with liquid. A slight movement of the diaphragm is magnified many times in the tube.

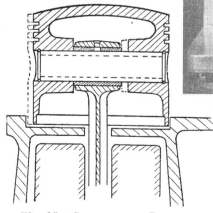

Fig. 15.—Centralising Piston in Spigot.

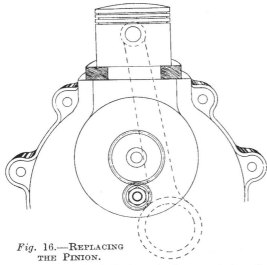

Fig. 16.—Replacing
the Pinion.

The piston should be brought down on to two flat blocks to enable the fixing nut to be tightened up. Position of rod shown is for unscrewing nut which is L.H. thread.

in direction of the piston, and broken rings result.

An Ingenious Instrument

Fig. 14 shows a very interesting instrument which is used in the factory for measuring the diameter of a piston at different points. Although this instrument is too elaborate for use in an ordinary repair shop, the principle is thought to be of sufficient interest to warrant the following description.

Essentially the apparatus consists of a surface plate having an upright arm attached to it. On the upright is carried the measuring appliance. The latter consists of a fine tube filled with liquid communicating on its lower end with a large flat circular vessel. The lower end of this vessel is closed by a flexible diaphragm with a pointer attached to the centre. The piston is placed on the surface plate, and the pointer adjusted so that it just touches the side of the piston as shown in Fig. 14. The piston can then be moved along underneath the pointer and also twisted round. Any variation in diameter will, of course, cause a slight movement of the pointer and diaphragm.

A simple calculation will show that if the diameter of the diaphragm is 3 inches and the internal diameter of the tube say one-tenth of an inch, the movement of the pointer will be magnified 900 times in the tube.

Valve Seatings, Guides and Springs

Valve seatings in cylinders should not be worn or badly pocketed. Valve-seating cutters can be obtained from the manufacturers, but new valve guides should first be fitted, as the pilot of the cutter would otherwise be loose and cut the seating out of alignment.

Valve guides must be replaced if any sign of wear is apparent, as heavy petrol consumption and erratic running can often be traced to this cause.

Valve springs can be inspected for loss of tension by placing a new one together with the old with ends butting in a vice (see Fig. 10). Screw up the vice, and if the old one closes up before the new one it is as well to renew it.

BIG ENDS AND GUDGEON BUSH

Assembling

Liners are replaced by pressing same in their housings. It is best to place a piece of flat metal underneath and either press or tap the liner until it is flush with side of rod. Great care must be exercised to see that the liner enters dead square, as if the alignment is bad a seized bearing will quickly result owing to the rollers tending to run up the crankpin. Small end can be replaced as shown in Fig. 7.

It may be found necessary to reamer out the bush after fitting same, as it will close in a little after drawing it in the housing.

Fig. 17.—REPLACING THE TIMING WHEELS.

Force the cam lever apart with the fingers as shown, and insert the timing wheel so that the centre-punch marks on the wheel and pinion correspond.

Having the crankpin in position in one side of flywheel, the rollers and cages can be put into correct position (see Fig. 5), and bearings placed over the crankpin. Place a little oil on all bearings before refitting parts.

Assembling Flywheels

If the connecting rod is from a twin engine be sure and place the inner rod the correct way. A small slot will be noted extending up the fork rod from the gash; this must be placed on the inside, so that the angle of the cylinders may be obtained (see Fig. 13). The fork is connected to the front cylinder. Now place other flywheel on the crankpin after having thoroughly cleaned the tapers with petrol for preference, in order to prevent any oil film remaining which might cause the flywheels to shift. Tighten up the flywheels in the flywheel block, but the outside diameters must be flush one with another for truing purposes. A very excellent little tool for this purpose is given in Fig. 11. It consists of a piece of round mild steel (which will go in between the flywheels) threaded at either end and two flat pieces of metal of about 5 inches long, 1½ inches wide and ⅝ inch thick, drilled in the centres to just clear the spindle, and two large nuts with the faces dead true with the thread.

If the spindle is placed in between the flywheels and the nuts tightened on the small blocks, the flywheels will be in most cases brought dead true and the crankpin nuts can be finally tightened.

Afterwards check them by revolving them in between lathe centres.

Fig. 18.—DISMANTLING A CYLINDER HEAD.
Note that a special angle box spanner must be used for undoing the fixing studs.

Assembling Flywheels in Crankcase

Now replace the roller bearing in driving side, the first roller cage being placed with the rollers facing the outside and back of cage facing towards flywheels. Then place the thick washer and after this the second cage of rollers, the back of cage facing the back of first cage. Now place the thin washer which butts against flywheel.

Place the flywheel in crankcase, and after placing the case in the vice on left-hand lugs and resting on wood block, fit a bolt in opposite lug and try for end play. There should be approximately ·008 inch, and any excess

can be taken up with shims on the driving-side. Do not move the
gear-side bush to take up the play, as this centralises the flywheels in
crankcase.

On some later type engines the driving side-bearings have no cages:
there are long rollers which must be packed in position with a little
grease.

Fitting Pistons

Refit the pistons according to the marks made on taking same off.
If of the end plug gudgeon type, the pins only require to be placed in the
piston, but on circlip type the circlips need to be replaced. Take care
to see that they are well bedded down in their grooves, or the pin may work
the circlips out and score the cylinder.

If a new gudgeon bush has been fitted, test the piston for being central
in the spigot of crankcase. This can be done by pushing the boss up
against the bush and noting the clearance between piston and spigot.
Repeat this operation on opposite side (see Fig. 15). Should this not be
central draw the gudgeon bush as necessary.

Fitting Cam Gear

Place the levers on their respective pivot pins: in the case of twin
engines with plain levers, the first lever to be fitted is the (1) rear inlet,
which goes on the front pivot pin, (2) front inlet on rear pivot pin, (3)
exhaust cam levers with the extension of pad facing outwards.

Pinion

Replace pinion on correct keyway. Bring piston down to rest on
block or two flat pieces of metal, and tighten up fixing nut (left-hand
thread).

Fitting Cam Wheel Exhaust Lifter and Drive

Now hold the levers apart with the fingers and place cam wheel in
bushes, noting that the centre-punch marks correspond on the pinion and
cam wheel. Place the distance piece over the lifter spindle. In some
engines the distance piece is fitted before the exhaust lifter and in others
the order is reversed. This is obvious by the position of lifter cam.

If new cam bushes have been fitted, the end play must be adjusted with
the cover in position: ·008 inch is allowed, but must be adjusted by shifting
the bushes in the drive. If new cam levers are fitted, see that the pads
are square on the cam faces by placing a little lamp black on the cams and
rotating engine.

Fit the chain or bevel drive with the exhaust lifter on the bearing.

Fig. 19.—Dismantling the Head.

First remove the push rods by levering the valves open.

and spindle protruding through the lifter guide hole in drive. As the drive is pushed over the studs, the lifter should be worked up and down to find the correct position for the lifter cam. It will slide on easily if care is taken to see that the cam is placed correctly to go between the lifter

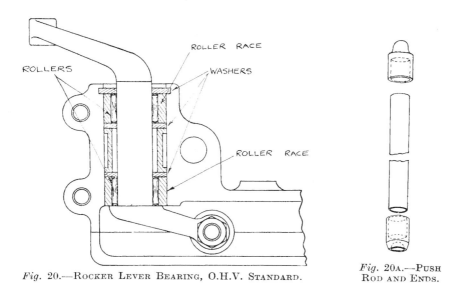

Fig. 20.—Rocker Lever Bearing, O.H.V. Standard.

Fig. 20a.—Push Rod and Ends.

heels on the cam levers. Before placing on cylinders put about half a teacupful of oil in the crankcase.

Cylinders

Fit on the cylinders and adjust the tappets to ·004 inch clearance inlet and ·006 inch exhaust. Fit the exhaust lifter spindle guide, replace washer, nut and brass nipple. Adjust the nut so that there is a full $\frac{1}{32}$ inch free movement of spindle before lifter heel engages with cam lever and lifts exhaust tappet.

Fig. 21.—Dismantling the Head.

After disconnecting the push rods unscrew rocker box fixing bolts and take off the rocker as shown above.

Valve Timing

The valve timing should be correct if the gear spindle has not been moved in the flywheels and instructions have been followed regarding replacement of pinion and cam wheel. Roughly, if the inlet valve opens slightly before top dead centre, the timing should be correct. In the case of engines with two separate cam wheels, take care to see that the front and rear inlets are not open at the same time.

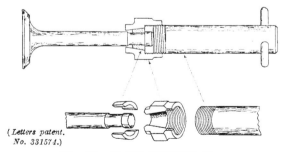

(*Letters patent.*
No. 331574.)

Fig. 22.—Valve Grinding Tool.

This cannot happen if they are replaced to the marks, but may do so if a new cam wheel is fitted.

Magneto Timing

Magneto sprockets and chain can now be refitted and timed so that the points on the contact breaker open when the piston is $\frac{7}{16}$ inch before top dead centre, piston going up on compression stroke and ignition lever fully advanced.

If bevel driven, the nut on bevel wheel on cam spindle is not tightened up, as it is necessary to get the piston in correct position, set the points on magneto just opening, then tap on the bevel with a brass punch and finally tighten the nut. Check over magneto timing afterwards to see that the bevel has not moved. With twin engines it is necessary to see

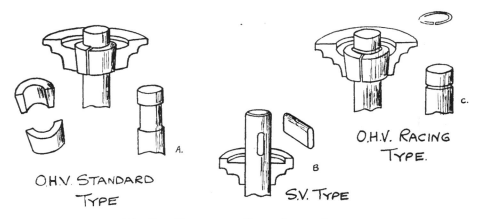

O.H.V. STANDARD TYPE

S.V. TYPE

O.H.V. RACING TYPE.

Fig. 23.—METHODS OF VALVE SPRING FIXING.

that No. 1 cam on magneto is timed to No. 1 cylinder. No. 1 cylinder is the left-hand one with cam gear facing forwards.

The complete valve and magneto timing for all types of engines is given on a separate chart.

OVERHEAD VALVE STANDARD ENGINES

The instructions given for the overhaul of side valve engines apply to the o.h.v., except for the difference on o.h.v. rocker gear and one or two small details.

Open Type Rocker Gear

To dismantle cylinder head a special angle box spanner is supplied for the fixing studs. It is a very difficult proposition to unscrew these studs without this spanner.

Dismantling Head

First remove the push rods by levering the valves open. Up to 1928 the bearings were of the plain bearing type, after which they were roller bearing. The hinge pin screws into one side of the standard and is plain on the opposite side. It is first necessary to take out the split pin, unscrew nut, then unscrew the hinge pin from rocker standard, a screwdriver slot being provided for this purpose.

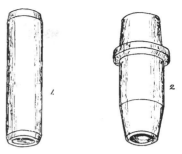

Fig. 24.—Valve Guides.

S.V. Type.   O.H.V. Type.

Do not attempt to drive out this pin after taking off the nut, otherwise a broken standard will result. In 1929 the enclosed rocker gear type was brought out.

To dismantle head first unscrew bell crank arm on front of rocker cover, take off cover. It is now possible to press down push rod cover, which will then pull forwards out of the spigot in rocker box. Disconnect push rods, and after taking off rocker fixing bolts the rocker box will be detached, leaving the head held by four bolts which can be taken out as explained previously. The rocker bearings will practically last as long as the engine. Do not worry about the endplay in rockers after dismantling the box, as this is positioned by the small pads on the rocker cover, therefore this must be in position when testing this.

If it should be more than a full $\frac{1}{64}$ inch, it can be adjusted by taking off the top half of the box and the roller races moved outwards, tightening the top half after adjusting.

In the direct attack type of push rod, the push rod rests in a recess in the cam lever, and there are no tappets. Be careful to see that the rods are replaced correctly with the loose ball engaging o.h. rocker.

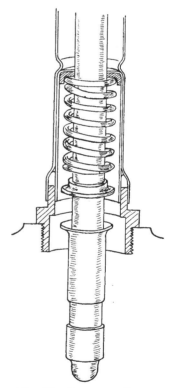

Fig. 25.—Push-rod Return Spring—O.H.V. Racing.

Taking out Valves

The valves are fitted with a split taper cone, and a tool is manufactured for taking these apart. It is similar to a carpenter's clamp, one end positioning under the valve head, the other resting on top of spring collar. This end is screwed, and by screwing same up it compresses the spring and the split cotters can be removed.   Upon releasing this, the collar and spring can be taken off.

Grinding Valves

No screwdriver slot is provided in the head of o.h.v. valves, as it is detrimental, but a special tool is sold by the manufacturers, Messrs. J. A. Prestwich, which will take any size of valve and is extremely simple to use (see Fig. 22).

The split cotters fitted to the valve stem are placed in the tool, and by screwing up the nut, the valve can be held in exactly the same manner as on the engine.

Cylinder Barrel

The barrel is held on the base in the same manner as the side-valve cylinders.

All other details are similar to the side-valve engines.

INTERESTING FITTING DETAILS ON SIDE-VALVE AND O.H.V. ENGINES

Push rod ends are renewed by tapping off the end cap from push rod and pressing on the new cap.   The detachable end is clearly shown by Fig. 20A.

When making up new complete push rods, care must be exercised when cutting the rod to length.   The method is to place the bottom end on the tappet, or in the case of enclosed rocker gear, on the recess in the cam lever, and place the loose top end cup in position at the side of the push rod, when it will be evident how much is required to cut off before fitting the end cup.

Previously it has been mentioned that it was possible to adjust the end-play in rockers by moving the race.   It will be clearly seen by Fig. 20 the position of the races in the rocker box.

On side-valve engines, valve guides are plain on the outside diameter and have no shoulders (see Fig. 24 (1)).   The correct position of these can be taken from the old guide.   When fitting these, which are a press fit in their housings, care must be exercised to see that they are not pressed in too far so that they foul the radius underneath valve head, or the valve will not seat.   There should be $\frac{3}{32}$-inch clearance between finish of radius and end of valve guide.

Racing type valve guides have a shoulder which locates the position (see Fig. 24 (2)).   Care is needed when tapping these in position.   Too much force will result in the shoulder being fractured.

When refitting the split cotters and collars to valves, see that they are placed on the same valves from which they were taken off, as they will be nicely bedded in, and it is therefore essential that they are kept together.   When fitting new split cotters they will be found to be split through one side, but only halfway through the opposite side.   They need to be sawn right through this side before fitting.   The reason they are delivered in this way is to be sure that the cone is a dead fit (see Fig. 23).

Side-valve Tappets

Tappets are supplied left long enough on the stem to take up wear. They therefore require to be cut off to correct length.   The old-type stems required hardening on the ends after cutting to length by heating to a cherry red and quenching in oil, but the latest type are hardened and only require grinding to length.

On racing valves of the latest type a spring ring is incorporated with the split cotters.   This is for locating the split cotters, and also acts as an extra safeguard for preventing the cotters moving.   This ring fits in a groove in the valve stem, and on its outside diameter rests in a recess provided in the split cotters (see Fig. 23c).   When dismantling the valve it is necessary to first remove the spring ring (after, of course, having compressed the spring), then the split cotters can be removed.

SPECIAL NOTES ON J.A.P. O.H.V. RACING ENGINES

Racing engines are manufactured in seven different types, comprising 175-c.c., 250-c.c., 350-c.c., 500-c.c., 600-c.c., 750-c.c. and 1,000-c.c. twin.

Compression Ratios

Pistons are supplied giving different compression ratios for petrol-benzol and alcohol fuels, and appended hereunder are suggested ratios for all engines.

			Piston for Petrol-Benzol.	Piston for Alcohol.
175 c.c.,	53	× 78 mm.	With $\frac{1}{8}''$ plate = 9 to 1 ratio	$\frac{1}{32}''$ plate = 13 to 1 ratio
250 c.c.,	62·5	× 80 mm.	No plate = 8·2 to 1 ,,	No plate = 10·4 to 1 ,,
350 c.c.,	70	× 90 mm.	No plate = 7·4 to 1 ,,	No plate = 10 to 1 ,,
500 c.c.,	80	× 99 mm.	$\frac{1}{16}''$ plate = 7 to 1 ,,	No plate = 10 to 1 ,,
600 c.c.,	85·7	× 104 mm.	$\frac{1}{8}''$ plate = 6·6 to 1 ,,	No plate = 8 to 1 ,,
750 c.c.,	74	× 85 mm.	$\frac{1}{8}''$ plate = 7 to 1 ,,	No plate = 8·25 to 1 ,,
1,000 c.c.,	80	× 99 mm.	$\frac{1}{16}''$ plate = 7 to 1 ,,	No plate = 10 to 1 ,,

Special Piston for 600 c.c. Engine

With the 600-c.c. single a special H.C. piston can be supplied, giving 12 to 1 ratio.   This, however, has been mainly used on the Continent for sidecar races.

Engine for Dirt-track Machines

There is also a special 500-c.c. dirt-track engine which has a bore and stroke of 80 × 99 mm. This engine is considerably lighter than the standard racing engine, weighing only 57 lb., and developing 36 B.H.P. on alcohol fuel.

Timing for Dirt-track Engine

The valve and magneto timing is given on the separate chart for all racing engines, but does not include the dirt-track engine.

This is as follows :

Inlet opens 39° before T.D.C. Inlet closes 64° after B.D.C.
Exhaust opens 66° before B.D.C. Exhaust closes 35° after T.D.C.
Magneto timing 37°, with ignition lever fully advanced.

Improving the Performance

There is very little work which can be put in to improve the performance of racing engines, as they are specially erected, and all the parts, such as ports, valves, head and piston crown are highly polished. It is necessary, however, when dismantling and re-erecting, to see that the parts are restored to their former condition by polishing the ports, head, valves, etc. Do not grind the valves unnecessarily with coarse grinding compound, but touch them up with a metal polish only, unless they are badly pitted on the seatings.

The piston ring clearance must not be as small in the gap as a standard engine, but should be about ·018 to ·020 for 60- and 70-mm. bores, and ·020 to ·025 for 80- and 85·7-mm. bore cylinders.

New copper gaskets should be fitted each time the head is taken off.

Regarding cam wheels, there are no special cams supplied other than those fitted to each engine.

Plugs

Recommended sparking plugs are :

KLG No. 348 or No. 341. The former stands more heat than the latter, but the latter will withstand more oil but less heat.

Lodge B.R. 19.

Carburetter Jets

Jet and choke sizes need considerable thought and experiment. It is impossible to lay down any hard-and-fast rule, but with a too large choke acceleration will suffer, and if too small the all-out speed will be restricted.

Too small a jet will quickly result in overheating and burnt exhaust valves, and with too large a jet the maximum revolution per minute will not be reached.

Transmission Parts

When tuning for racing the engine very often receives all the attention, and vital parts, such as gearbox, wheel bearing, tension of chains, etc., are neglected. It is essential to have these parts free running, as a good deal of loss of speed can be traced to tightness in these fitments.

Gear Ratios

Gear ratios need a good deal of thought, and it is found in most cases that one is apt to overgear. This is very detrimental, as the engine can never reach its peak revolutions per minute.

For ordinary races, such as on give-and-take roads, the following gear ratios will be found about the best for solo work:

175-c.c.	250-c.c.	350-c.c.	500-c.c.	600-c.c.	750-c.c.	1,000-c.c.
7·3 to 1	6 to 1	5·3 to 1	4·25 to 1	4·25 to 1	4 to 1	3·25 to 1

Hereunder is a chart giving engine revolutions at various road speeds and gear ratios for 26-inch diameter road wheels.

Gear : 3½	3¾	4	4¼	4½	4¾	5	5¼	5½	5¾	6	6¼
m.p.h.					Engine	Revolutions	per	minute			
5	226	242	258	275	291	307	323	339	355	372	388	404
10	452	484	517	549	581	614	646	679	711	743	776	808
15	679	727	775	824	872	921	1,018	1,066	1,115	1,163	1,212
20	905	969	1,034	1,099	1,163	1,228	1,293	1,358	1,422	1,486	1,551	1,616
25	1,131	1,212	1,292	1,373	1,454	1,535	1,616	1,697	1,777	1,858	1,939	2,020
30	1,357	1,454	1,551	1,648	1,745	1,842	1,939	2,036	2,133	2,230	2,327	2,424
35	1,583	1,697	1,810	1,923	2,036	2,149	2,262	2,376	2,488	2,602	2,715	2,828
40	1,810	1,938	2,068	2,198	2,326	2,456	2,586	2,716	2,844	2,972	3,102	3,232
45	2,036	2,182	2,327	2,470	2,617	2,763	2,909	3,055	3,200	3,345	3,490	3,636
50	2,262	2,424	2,585	2,747	2,908	3,070	3,232	3,394	3,555	3,716	3,878	4,040
55	2,488	2,666	2,844	3,022	3,199	3,370	3,555	3,733	3,910	4,087	4,265	4,444
60	2,715	2,908	3,102	3,296	3,490	3,684	3,878	4,072	4,266	4,460	4,654	4,848
65	2,941	3,150	3,360	3,570	3,781	3,991	4,201	4,411	4,621	4,831	5,042	5,252
70	3,167	3,394	3,620	3,846	4,072	4,298	4,524	4,752	4,976	5,204	5,430	5,656
75	3,394	3,636	3,878	4,121	4,362	4,605	4,847	5,091	5,331	5,576	5,818	6,060
80	3,620	3,876	4,136	4,396	4,652	4,912	5,172	5,432	5,688	5,944	6,204	6,464
85	3,846	4,118	4,394	4,671	4,943	5,219	5,495	5,771	6,043	6,316	6,588	6,868
90	4,072	4,364	4,654	4,940	5,234	5,526	5,818	6,110	6,400	6,690	6,980	7,272
95	4,299	4,606	4,912	5,214	5,525	5,833	6,141	6,449	6,755	7,061	7,367	7,676
100	4,525	4,848	5,170	5,494	5,816	6,140	6,464	6,788	7,110	7,432	7,756	8,080

In conjunction with above chart a suitable gear can be selected by studying where the engine peaks, as follows :

Engine	.	.	175-c.c.	250-c.c.	350-c.c.	500-c.c.	600-c.c.	750-c.c.	1,000-c.c.
R.P.M.	.	.	7,000	6,500	6,200	5,600	5,200	5,500	5,200
Brake horse-power		12	17·3	23	31	33	40	58

For 28-inch wheels multiply the revolutions by ·93, and for 24-inch wheels multiply by 1·03.

VALVE AND VALVE GUIDE REPAIRS

By Lieut.-Colonel D. J. Smith, O.B.E., M.I.A.E.

WHEN the engine is dismantled after considerable running, having had the valves ground in and the cylinder, etc., decarbonised several times, wear begins to be evident even if it has not made itself obvious in the running of the engine. Probably on the last occasion when the valves were ground in, wear on the valve stems and in the guides was noticed; now it is much more pronounced.

Inlet or Exhaust Stem and Guide Wear equally Important

It is often thought that only wear in the inlet valve stem and guide is really of importance, but this is not so. It is true that wear of the inlet valve guide and stem makes starting difficult and slow running very irregular and jerky, but wear in the exhaust valve guide and stem, although it is not evident in the running, is of equal importance, as it will in time ruin the valve seating in the head or cylinder.

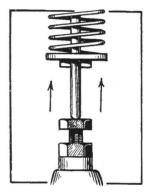

Fig. 1.—Ordinary Straight Lift Push Rod and Valve Stem.

No side pressure on valve stem.

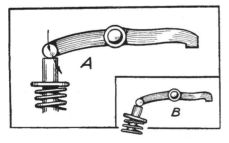

Fig. 2.—Overhead Valve.

A, note semicircular path swept by end of rocker arm tending to deflect valve stem as at B. Exaggerated.

Repair in Good Time

Valve stem and guide wear is much more pronounced in engines having overhead valves and employing no tappets than in the ordinary side-by-side valve engines. This will be seen from Figs. 1 and 2 A and B. With the tappet, the valve stem gets a perfectly straight lift. With the valve stem operated by the rocker arm, as in Fig. 2, there is some side pressure given to the valve stem which causes extra wear. The appearance of a valve seat, where considerable play in the guide has existed, is shown in Fig. 3. The wear may appear slight, but it

184

Fig. 2a.—Assembling the Valve Guides in a Motor-cycle Engine (B.S.A.).

Although it is permissible to use a mild steel tube for driving the valve guide home, as shown above, no attempt should be made to dislodge a tight valve guide in this manner. The correct method is shown in Fig. 9.

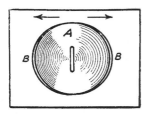

Fig. 3.—SEATING WORN OVAL THROUGH PLAY IN VALVE GUIDE.

A, Head of valve. BB, Oval wear of seating. Valve head has had a slight movement in direction of arrows.

needs a considerable amount of regrinding to put it right, and if it is allowed to continue in this state it may get beyond the grinding stage and need recuttering, or in extreme cases a new seating fitted in the head, or the old seat built up by welding and recuttered.

In some cases of overhead valves the seating is detachable, and is solid with the guide. This is quite a good system, although of very old design (Fig. 4), as the seat and guide form an inexpensive item, and in event of wear can be replaced with new, with the advantage of a narrow seating which cannot be obtained with the ordinary solid seating, which gets wider each time the valve is ground or cuttered in.

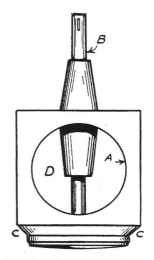

Fig. 4.—DETACHABLE VALVE SEAT AS USED ON SOME OVERHEAD VALVE ENGINES.

A, Seating. B, Valve. CC, Coned seating of seat in cylinder casting. D, Port for passage of gases.

How to remove the Guide

The first case to be considered is a solid-head cylinder (Fig. 5). The valve guides have been pressed in by the makers and are a tight fit; this fit has also been increased by the heat to which the guides have been exposed, especially the exhaust valve guides. Cast iron, of which these guides are made, has the property of "growing" when exposed to extreme heat (Fig. 6), and in some cases the top of the guide projecting into the valve pocket (Fig. 6) has increased in diameter until it cannot be forced back through the hole in the cylinder casting. Where the guide is well tapered off at the upper end (Fig. 7), this is not likely to occur. While the old guide can sometimes be safely driven out of a water-cooled cylinder by the aid of a block of copper or bronze and a hammer (Fig. 8), this must not be tried with an air-cooled cylinder, or it will probably be smashed, or in any case have fins broken off. The correct treatment is shown in Fig. 9.

Fig. 5.—SOLID HEAD SIDE-BY-SIDE VALVE CYLINDER.

A, Valve guides (Royal Enfield).

Procure a length of iron gas or water pipe, or weldless drawn steel tube is better, large enough in inside diameter to go easily over the flange on the valve guide (B, Fig. 9), and long enough to allow the guide to be drawn right out of its seat. The tube should be cut quite square on each end, and if it has been sawn off to length with a hacksaw, can be filed square on the ends afterwards. A bolt is now required of a diameter which will pass through the guide and long enough to go through both guide and tube (C, Fig. 9). Ordinary stock bolts are seldom to be had of this length, and also would not be of good enough material to stand the strain; an ordinary $\frac{5}{16}$-inch diameter bolt is easily twisted off.

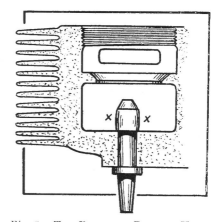

Fig. 6.—Top Parallel Part of Valve Guide " Grown " by Heat.

The growth is shown exaggerated at X X. It prevents the guide being forced out.

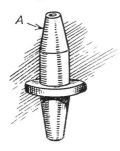

Fig. 7.—Valve Guide.

Top of guide well tapered off at A, where it is exposed in valve pocket.

Procure a length of silver steel of the right diameter: it is sold in 12-inch lengths at a few pence per length. Anneal this by heating to a bright red heat, and then burying in the ashes under the fire or in a box of lime to cool off. Cut off the length required with a hacksaw, and then screw it at both ends, one end just long enough to take the nut, the other for about threequarters the length of the guide (Fig. 10). Put a nut on the short screw end, and drop the other end through the guide. Then slip the tube over the guide, put a stout washer over the bolt and the end of the tube, and screw up. Put a good strain on with the nut, and note if guide moves. If not, take a piece of

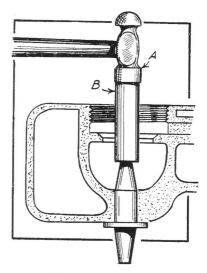

Fig. 8.—Not this with Air-cooled Cylinder.

Valve guide of water-cooled cylinder being driven out by copper drift and hammer. Very liable to damage cylinder casting of an air-cooled cylinder.

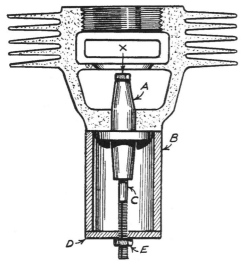

Fig. 9.—METHOD OF WITHDRAWING VALVE GUIDE.

A, Guide. B, Length of steel tube. C, Bolt or long stud. D, stout washer. E, nut. Tightening nut E draws out guide. To start the guide a smart tap on the head of the bolt at X is sometimes necessary.

brass or copper rod, and with a hammer give the bolt head on the top of guide a smart blow as in Fig. 8. This will probably start the guide, and it can then be forced out with the bolt.

If Removal is Difficult

If it is still obstinate, drop the cylinder head downwards in a bucket of paraffin, and allow to soak for an hour or so, and try again. While this work is being done on the cylinder, it should be held on the wood block as shown in Fig. 3, Decarbonising your Motor-cycle, see page 47. Otherwise the cylinder is liable to fall over or on the floor and sustain damage. If there is no vice available, bolt the cylinder down to the bench by the flange (Fig. 11), and it will be quite firm to work upon. If silver steel is not procurable for the bolt, a good brand of bright drawn mild steel can be used, while if no screwing tackle is available, a Newall Hi-tensile bolt of the length required can be purchased from such firms as Buck and Hickmann, Whitechapel, London, or Geo. Adams, Holborn, London. These bolts are about two and a half times the strength of ordinary steel bolts (Fig. 12).

Fig. 10.—TOOL FOR WITHDRAWING GUIDE.

As the bolt shown in Fig. 9 is generally over stock length, it may be necessary to make one up out of silver or bright drawn mild steel: the former is preferable. Screw it at A just long enough to take the nut, and at B long enough to allow guide to be drawn out of its seat.

Inserting the New Guide

When the old guide is drawn out, the new guide is inserted by transferring the tube and washer to the valve pocket (Fig. 13), and drawing it in. Before inserting it, well coat the outside of the guide and the inside of its hole with flake graphite, and it will be able to be removed when required without trouble.

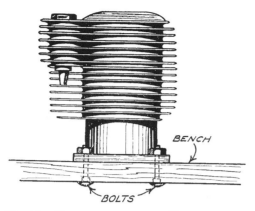

Fig. 11.—Cylinder bolted to Bench to hold it firm while being worked upon.

Fig. 12.—Newall Hi-Tensile Bolt.

About $2\frac{1}{2}$ times the strength of ordinary steel bolts.

In Very Obstinate Cases

The valve guides in the cylinder head for overhead valves are dealt with in the same manner. In the case of a valve guide which cannot be removed by ordinary methods owing to "growing" (see Fig. 6) or rusting, proceed as follows. Bolt the cylinder by the flange to the table of a drilling machine (Fig. 14), and then with a drill about $\frac{1}{16}$ inch diameter less than that of the body of the guide drill it out. The thin shell left by the drill can then be easily removed by chipping it out with a small cross-cut chisel.

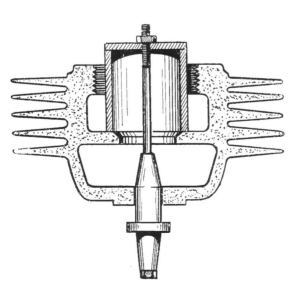

Fig. 13.—Valve Guide being drawn into its Seating. Using same methods as in Fig. 9.

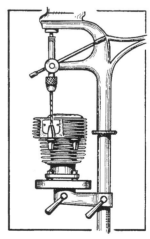

Fig. 14.—The Last Resort.

Showing guide being drilled out on drilling machine when it cannot be removed by other methods. Drill should be about $\frac{1}{16}$ inch less than diameter of body of guide.

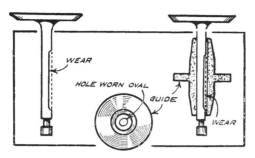

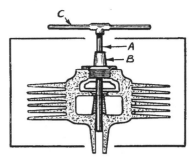

Fig. 15.—VALVE AND GUIDE WORN.

Although the wear of the guide and the valve are each slight, the combined amount of wear causes extensive leak and allows head of valve to move on seating, causing this to wear oval (see Fig. 3).

Fig. 16.—VALVE GUIDE CAST SOLID WITH CYLINDER BEING REAMERED OUT TO RESTORE TRUTH.

A, Reamer. B, Guide for reamer screws in valve plug hole. C, Handle for turning reamer.

The hole is then cleaned of rust, and the new guide can be inserted. The guide can be drilled out by a breast drill, as the hole for the valve spindle acts as a guide for the drill, so that it cannot run out of truth.

Fig. 17.—VALVE FORGING OR STAMPING.

In 3 per cent. nickel steel. Can be machined to suit non-standard guides and seatings.

Fitting Valve to New Guide

When the new guide is fitted, insert the valve and grind it in in the usual manner. Generally, by the time the guide is worn enough to need removal, the valve stem is also worn, and it pays to fit a new valve at the same time as a new guide (Fig. 15). Reamers are sold to enable valve guides to be trued up in place, but this means a valve with a larger stem, non-standard, which would have to be made specially, so there would be no advantage. In a few cases the valve guides are solid with the cylinder or head, and it is then worth while reamering them out to obtain a true hole, and fitting a valve with a stem to suit. A reamer for this work is shown in Fig. 16, while valve forgings (Fig. 17) can be obtained in a large variety of sizes and can be turned up to suit the guide and seat. This may have to be done in the case of a very badly burned or worn valve seating, where it is impossible to use a valve of the original diameter

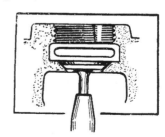

Fig. 18.—FIT AN OVERSIZE VALVE.

A badly burned seating which, to restore truth, has had to be cuttered out so that a standard valve is useless. Standard valve shown in seating. Remedy, oversize valve must be fitted.

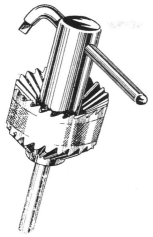

Fig. 19.—Combined Valve and Seating Cutter.

The outer cone is for the seating and the inner for the valve. Various size pilots and bushes can be fitted to suit different diameters of stems.

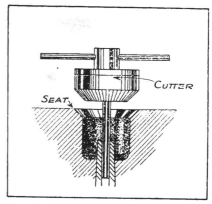

Fig. 19a.—A Cheaper Type of Cutter.
This deals with one size seating only.
Will not reface the valves.

(Fig. 18), so a special valve is turned up for it.

Valve-seat Cutters

In such cases, and in very badly burned or worn seatings, a valve cutter is necessary to restore the seat to truth before grinding in. There are several such tools, but one of the best is shown in Fig. 19. This is a double-purpose tool, the outside of the cone dealing with the seating and the inside with the valve.

Collets and guides are provided, so that valves with several sizes of stems can be dealt with. Such tools are expensive, and would

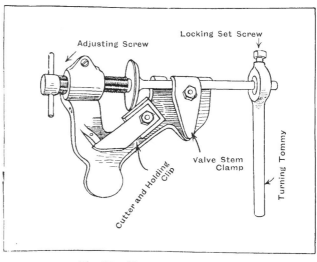

Fig. 20.—Valve-truing Tool.
Will take any size of valve, and cutter can be adjusted to any angle.

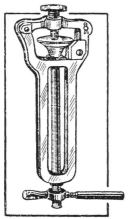

Fig. 20A.—ANOTHER TYPE OF VALVE TRUING TOOL.

Restricted as regards size of valves with which it can deal.

only be warranted in cases where a good number of repairs of this type are dealt with. A very fine result is given, however, and only the very smallest amount of grinding is necessary after the valve and seating have been dealt with by these cutters.

Valve-truing Tools

For truing the valves only, a tool like Fig. 20 is a very good investment, as it only costs 8s. 8d. In no case must grinding be resorted to to rectify a badly worn valve; it must be cuttered to truth first, or the valve seating in the head or cylinder will be practically worn out in restoring the valve to truth, and if no cutter is available it is cheaper in such cases to fit a new valve.

Building up the Seat by Welding

Where the seating in the head or cylinder is in a very bad state, it is often possible to build up the metal by welding, and then machine up a new seat, either by mounting the job in the lathe or cuttering it up with a tool as in Figs. 19 and 19A. In Fig. 21 is shown the three stages in such a process, but each case must be judged on its merits, as such a repair is not possible in all cases.

Before cutting the Seat

The practice, often resorted to in water-cooled engines, of boring out the old seat and fitting in a collar on which the new seat is formed (Fig. 22) cannot often be resorted to in air-cooled engines owing to the lack of metal

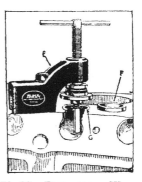

Fig. 22.—REPLACING A WORN SEATING ON A WATER-COOLED ENGINE.

The old seating is bored out and a new seat ring seen on top of cylinder block on right is pressed in as shown, and the seating is then cuttered in it. In most air-cooled engines there would be insufficient metal to allow of this repair being carried out.

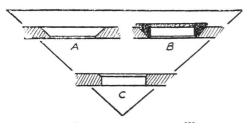

Fig. 21.—SEATING BUILT UP BY WELDING.

Showing seating worn too far for use A, built up by electric welding B, and new seating cuttered in C.

to enable this to be done. Before using any of the cutters shown in Figs. 19A, 20 and 20A to true a valve, the hard scale which forms on the seat should first be removed or the cutters will soon be blunted. This can be done by lightly filing the seats with an old smooth file (Fig. 23), or holding the valve seat against a grinding wheel very lightly and revolving it with the fingers until

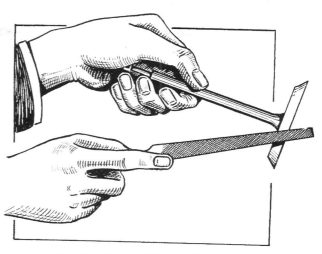

Fig. 23.—Before Truing Valve.

The hard scale must be removed from the seat with a fine file used very lightly.

the scale is all ground off (Fig. 24). On some engines persistent hanging up of the exhaust valve is often attributed to a bent valve stem. While a bent stem would cause this trouble, it is much more often due to a distorted guide, assuming, of course, that it is not caused by scale or carbon deposited on the stem.

Truing Distorted Guide

The guides are machined when cold, and then forced into their places, where the top ends are subjected, in the case of exhaust valves, to a very high temperature. The result (exaggerated) is shown in Fig. 25. To remedy this a reamer should be put through the

Fig. 24.—Another Method.

Hold seat of valve lightly against revolving emery wheel and turn valve with fingers to bring all the seat on the wheel.

Fig. 25. — VALVE GUIDE DISTORTED BY HEAT.

This causes binding of valve stem.

guide which will true up the hole. A $\frac{5}{16}$-inch parallel reamer can be purchased for 2*s*. 6*d*., and will be useful for other purposes. After reamering out the guide, the valve must be ground in to ensure that any alteration due to the reamering out of the guide is corrected. A $\frac{5}{16}$-inch reamer is only mentioned as an example. Reamers can be purchased in sizes varying by $\frac{1}{64}$ inch, so that one the size of the valve stem can always be obtained.

Replacing the Exhaust Valve

When replacing the exhaust valve, polish the stem well with graphite, and it will prevent scale forming, and reduce the liability of the valve hanging up. Oil is of no use at the temperature at which these valves operate; it is merely carbonised, and aggravates the trouble.

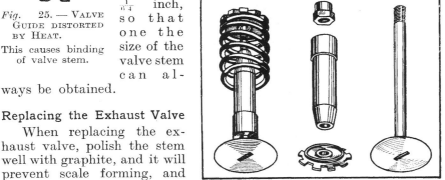

Fig. 26.—A VALVE STEM WITHOUT COTTER.

End of valve stem is threaded and toothed spring washer is screwed on and locked by hardened steel nut seen above the valve guide (Douglas).

On some engines a grease-gun nipple is provided on the inlet valve guide. In this case there is little heat, and the grease performs an important duty in keeping the valve guide airtight, even if slightly worn, and so assisting starting. The casing in of valve guides, springs and stems in side-by-side valve engines is a great help in reducing troubles from hung up valves, as dirt and dust are excluded, and the springs, tappets, etc., are assured of a supply of oil. This more than compensates for the loss of accessibility due to the casing in of these parts.

Special Note on Douglas Type Stem and Guide

In some cases no valve cotters are used, the spring washer is screwed on to the end of the valve stem, and a hardened steel nut is used to lock it, the nut also taking the thrust of the

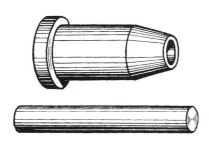

Fig. 27.—VALVE TAPPET AND TAPPET GUIDE (DOUGLAS).

push rod. This is clearly seen from Fig. 26, which shows the Douglas valve and guide. In tightening up the nut and washer on the end of

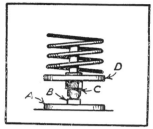

Fig. 28.—VALVE AND PUSH ROD, SHOWING CLEARANCE ADJUSTMENT BY HARDENED STEEL NUT SCREWED ON END OF VALVE.

The push rod is plain, as in Fig. 27. A, Guide. B, Push rod. C, Hardened steel nut. D, Spring washer.

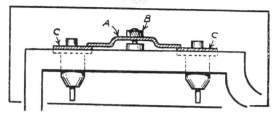

Fig. 29.—METHOD OF HOLDING PUSH-ROD GUIDES ON DOUGLAS ENGINES.

A, Spring clip. B, Nut holding clip. CC, Push-rod guides. By removing clip A guides can be lifted out.

these valves, discretion must be used, or the valve stem may be broken, or the thread stripped or stretched. In some cases, using this type of construction, the nut is used as a means of adjusting the clearance instead of the valve tappet, which in these cases is just a plain rod (Fig. 27). It is really a reversal of the usual system (Fig. 28). The valve-stem nut must be very firmly tightened up, but this must not be overdone.

In the Douglas engine the tappet guides are readily detachable (Fig. 29), and when worn are quite inexpensive to renew, the tappet also (Fig. 27) is simply a plain length of round steel suitably hardened. If desired the tappet guide can be reamered out when worn and a new tappet fitted. To make this, cut off a suitable length of silver steel of the correct diameter after the guide hole has been reamered, and see that the ends of the rod are dead true and square. If a lathe is available, the ends can be faced up, the rod being held in a self-centering chuck. Then heat the length to a bright cherry-red heat, and dip out in cold water. Then polish it with fine emery cloth, and holding it in a pair of tongs or pliers, heat over the flame of a blow-

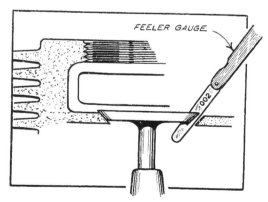

Fig. 30.—RESULT OF USING VALVE SEAT CUTTERS WITH PLAY IN THE PILOT OR STEM AND VALVE GUIDE.

Seating is not true with guide, and a feeler gauge can be got between valve and seating.

lamp or a Bunsen gas burner. Watch the polished surface carefully, and when it turns a light straw colour plunge the rod into cold water. This will give a temper too hard to wear or " jump up " at the ends, yet not hard enough to chip. Repairs to the ordinary types of push rods and guides will be dealt with under crank chamber repairs.

BENT VALVES

Occasionally, due to something lodging under the seat or to mis-handling, valve stems get bent.

Actually, the best thing to do is to scrap the valve and fit a new one, but as valves generally cost about 5s. each, it may be considered worth while straightening them. This can be done as follows. First see that the stem is an easy fit in its valve guide. If the guide is worn and going to be replaced so much the better, as it can then be reamered out a fairly slack fit to the spindle, so that there is a certain amount of shake.

Lay the valve on a bed of coke or asbestos " coals " on a brazing hearth, if one is available, or on any iron plate if not, and blow the valve a bright red heat all over with a blowpipe or blowlamp. Then pick it up quickly by the stem with a pair of pliers or tongs, and drop it on its seat.

With a block of wood, about the same diameter as the head of valve, and a hammer, give the head several smart quick taps to seat it accurately. Allow to cool out, and when removed it will be true, and can be ground in as usual when the new guide has been fitted.

Owing to the expansion of the valve stem by heat, it is very probable that it would not go through the guide if it was unworn, but if in doubt, heat the stem of the valve alone first, and try it in the guide ; some of the steels used for valves have an extremely low coefficient of expansion, and would still pass through the guide even when redhot. If the guide is in good order and is to be retained, polish it inside with flake graphite, using a swab to do this (see Valve Grinding and Decarbonising), and there will be no fear of the stem sticking in the guide or damaging it.

When using the valve-seating cutters (Figs. 19 and 19A), there is a very important point which must be observed. The stems or pilots must be a good fit in the valve guides or the seat will not be cuttered true to the guide, and no amount of grinding will correct it. If a new valve guide is to be fitted, fit it before cuttering the seat. There must be no appreciable shake in the cutter stem when in the guide. If this rule is not observed, it will often be found possible to slip a feeler gauge of say ·002 inch under the valve head for a good part of its circumference (Fig. 30) when the valve is dropped into its place, showing that the seating is not true with the guide.

INDEX

INDEX

INDEX

INDEX

Motorcycles in a Nutshell
Capt S Bramley-Moore 1923
184 pages and Numerous illustrations

The Petrol Engine,-Construction of the Engine-The Timing of the Valves- Engine Lubrication-The Two Stroke Engine-Carburettor-Magneto-Clutch-Gearbox-Frame and Brakes-Sidecars-Lighting-Hints on Driving-Tuning up the Machine-Faults and Troubles-Index

£25 plus Postage £3.30 UK 5.60 Europe, £7.99 Australia, NZ, USA Rest of the World

Now Avaiable from classicmotorcyclemanuals.com paypal to stevearch58@hotmail.com 01684 567 231
1 Arley House 5 Hanley Terrace Malvern Wells WR14 4PF

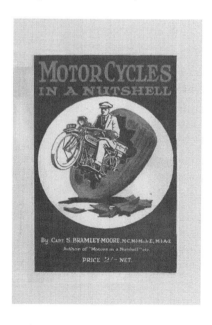

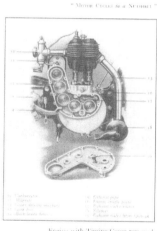

Engine with Timing Cover removed, showing gear-driven Magneto

Feedback
'Fast delivery to Australia, high quality book, many thanks'

The Motor Cyclist's Handbook 1911 by Phoenix

Written by a young motorcycle engineer for the layman in 1911 this profusely illustrated book is an absolute joy for anyone interested in the development, design and the maintenance of veteran motorcycles. A great piece of Social history reproduced as a good quality hardback book for your enjoyment. Full of references to, or adverts for Chater Lea, Douglas, Montgomery, Triumph, Hobart, IVY, NSU, Peugeot, Rex, Premier, JAP, Scott, Arno, Norton, NSU, Motor Reve, BAT, FN, Wanderer, Zenith Motorcycles, AMAC, B & B, JAP and Longuemare Carbs, Bosch Magnetos, Jones Speedo, Dunhill Acetylene Lights, Armstrong Triplex Three speed Gear.

Feedback

'Everyone at the shop impressed by the book (Veralls)'.
Ian Hatton

Hi Steve, The book has arrived safely today, highly delighted, thanks. Jim L. Dunblane

'I just received my copy and enjoyed it so much, that the one I have just purchased I would like to send to my frie nd...............'   Zac
Bermuda